D0600198

PARTY CAKES
for kids

©Murdoch Books Pty Limited 2006.
This 2007 edition published by Barnes & Noble, Inc.
by arrangement with Murdoch Books Pty Limited.

All rights reserved. No part of this publication may be reproduced, stored
in a retrieval system, or transmitted, in any form or by any means, electronic,
mechanical, photocopying, recording, or otherwise, without prior written
permission from the publisher.

Photographers: Ian Hofstetter (openers and cover), Oliver Ford
Stylists: Jane Collins (openers and cover), Carolyn Fienberg
Templates: Steve Pollitt

ISBN-13: 978-0-7607-8970-4
ISBN-10: 0-7607-8970-3

Printed and bound by Midas Printing (Asia) Ltd. Printed in CHINA.

1 3 5 7 9 10 8 6 4 2

IMPORTANT: Those who might be at risk from the effects of salmonella poisoning (the elderly, pregnant women, young children, and those suffering from immune deficiency diseases) should consult their doctor with any concerns about eating raw eggs.

CONVERSION GUIDE: You may find cooking times vary depending on the oven you are using. For convection ovens, as a general rule, set the oven temperature to 70°F lower than indicated in the recipe. We have used 20 ml (4 teaspoon) tablespoon measures. If you are using a 15 ml (3 teaspoon) tablespoon, for most recipes the difference will not be noticeable. However, for recipes using baking powder, gelatin (jello), baking soda, or small amounts of cornstarch, add an extra teaspoon for each tablespoon specified.

PARTY CAKES
for kids

KATHY KNUDSEN

BARNES
& NOBLE

NEW YORK

contents

before you start

A birthday cake is the centerpiece of every birthday party, but it should be simple enough so that there is plenty of time and energy left for planning the party. Our aim has been to create cakes that spark your child's imagination and are within easy reach of busy parents. All the cakes can be made with package cake mix and easy-to-find decorations. As for the techniques, they are simple enough for the home cook to do with relative ease. Read below for all the basics and tips of the trade that will help turn cake decorating into a trouble-free (and fun) experience!

The best (and most logical) place to begin is the cake recipe itself as it covers everything you need to know about the cake. It is a good idea to familiarize yourself with the recipe at least a few days before the birthday party to make sure that you have everything.

cake pans

It might seem obvious, but it is essential that you use the right pan(s) for each cake. All the cooking times, quantities, and templates have been based on the pans specified in the recipes. You will find the necessary pan(s) listed in the equipment list for each cake. To find out the size of a pan, turn it upside down and measure across the middle of the base with a ruler. The pans used in this book are fairly standard ones and are available at large supermarkets and department stores. If you do have trouble, try a kitchenware store.

caring for your pans Most standard pans are made from aluminium, while the more unusual-shaped pans are made from specially treated tin. If yours are made from tin, dry them completely before storing or they will rust.

greasing and lining pans To stop the cake sticking to the pans during cooking, grease and line them before baking. First, cut baking parchment to the shape of the base of the pans. Next, grease your pans with either melted butter or oil—apply it evenly but not too thickly with a pastry brush, taking care to coat the corners. Vegetable-oil sprays may also be used; apply in a well-ventilated area away from any heat source. After greasing, line your pan with the piece of baking parchment you have cut. If you don't have paper, sprinkle the greased pan with all-purpose flour, turning the pan to coat the base and sides evenly. Shake off any excess flour by gently tapping the upturned pan.

the basic cakes

All the cakes in this book have been made using 11¾-ounce packages of butter cake mix. If you are using a package cake mix check the size of the package you are using and adjust the measurements accordingly—you will also have to consider the different measurements if more than one cake mix is required.

But you need not feel limited to butter cake—other plain cake mixes, such as chocolate, will work just as well. If you want to make your own, see the recipes on page 10.

baking the cakes Once the cake mix is made, pour it into the pan, then smooth the surface and bake in the center of the oven. If you have a convection oven, reduce your oven temperature by 50–70°F as it is hotter than a conventional oven.

cooking times Many of the party cakes use more than one package cake, so we have based the cooking times on the assumption that both cakes will be cooked at the same time, unless otherwise stated in the recipe. Where possible, bake the cakes on the same shelf of the oven without the pans touching. If your oven isn't large enough to fit both on one shelf, cook them on separate shelves on either side of the oven. Of course, you can also cook them one at a time; if so, see the package for the cooking time. Because there are so many variables, we give a span in the cooking times—you should check the cakes at the earlier time.

when is the cake cooked?

A cake is cooked when it begins to shrink away from the side of the pan. A skewer inserted into the center of the cake should come out clean—if not, return the cake to the oven until it is cooked through. Do not test a cake through a crack as this may give an incorrect result.

A cake is quite fragile when removed from the oven so leave it in the pan for 5–10 minutes to firm up, before turning onto a wire rack to cool completely. If the cake seems to be stuck, gently run a flat-bladed knife around the side to release the cake. Gently peel away the lining paper immediately.

ahead of time

Making the base cakes ahead of time not only means less for you to do on the party day itself, but it also minimizes crumbs sticking to the frosting when you are decorating. Transfer the cooled cake to an airtight container and store in a cool place for up to 3 days, or freeze for up to 3 months. If freezing, thaw for 2 hours before decorating. If you do make the cake on the day, allow it to cool completely before you decorate it.

cake boards

You will need a cake plate or cake board to support the cake, not only when you are serving, but also while you are decorating, because if you move the cake once it is decorated you risk cracking the frosting or breaking the cake. Cake boards can be made from masonite or a similar strong board which has been wrapped in paper. A non-absorbent paper is the best as the oils from the cake and frosting can seep into absorbent paper and leave an unattractive mark.

covering cake boards

To cover a square or rectangular board, cut a piece of paper 2 inches larger than the board. Cut into the corners, then fold the paper over the edge of the cake board and tape it to the underside of the board. To cover a round cake board, place the board on an upside-down piece of paper. Draw around the board, then draw an outline 2 inches larger than the board. Cut out the paper following the larger outline. Make cuts to the smaller outline about 1/2 inch apart. Replace the board in the center of the paper and then fold the cut edges over. Secure the paper to the bottom of the board with tape.

which way up?

Once the cake is cool and the cake board is covered, the next step is to prepare the cake. In most cases, it is best to have the top side of the cake facing up, as the baked smooth surface makes it easier to see any markings you might have to make.

However, sometimes you will need to level cakes, either to remove a dome to give a flat surface, or to make two adjoining cakes the same level. If so, invert the cakes, as the uncut surface is easier to frost. Cakes should be leveled with a serrated knife—the teeth on serrated knives give a sharper cutting action than most flat-bladed knives.

All of our party cakes have been double-tested by our team of home economists. When we test our cakes, we rate them for ease of preparation. The following ratings are on the cakes in this book, making them easy to use and understand.

 A single cupcake indicates a cake that is simple and relatively quick to make— perfect for beginners.

 Two cupcakes indicate the need for just a little more care and some more time.

 Three cupcakes indicate party cakes that require a greater investment in time, care, and patience—but the results are well worth it.

joining cakes

If your party cake uses more than one base cake, you will need to join them. Place the undecorated, cooled, and trimmed cakes on the cake board and use frosting or warm jam to join them. If you have to join two cakes that sit on top of one another, never use toothpicks: they can get lost and may accidentally be served to a child. Use skewers because they are more obvious and easy to remove before serving.

how to use the templates

Some of the cakes have a template to help you cut and decorate the cake. The templates are very easy to use, especially if you have access to a photocopier. Photocopy your chosen template from the back of the book and enlarge it by the percentage given to achieve the desired size. If the enlarged image is greater than your copy paper, you may need to increase the size over several areas of the image, then piece the paper together using adhesive tape. It's a good idea to do more than one copy just in case you make any mistakes.

If you don't have access to a photocopier, draw a graph with squares the size indicated under the template, then transfer the image onto the larger graph.

Once you have your template copied, cut it out, sit it on the cake, then secure it at a few anchor points with toothpicks to prevent the template moving when cutting. Some of the templates have features that need to be transferred onto the cake. To do this, pierce through the paper with a skewer or toothpick.

making the frosting

We have used three different types of frosting to decorate our cakes: buttercream, meringue frosting and white chocolate ganache. See page 11 for the recipes.

food colorings

In most cases, the frosting will need to be colored—you can use powdered, liquid, and paste food colorings, which can be purchased from cake-decorating suppliers, supermarkets, large craft and fabric stores, and some health food stores. For darker or bolder colors such as black, navy, or red, it is best to use powders or pastes as they give a much truer color than liquid.

powders and pastes Powdered food colorings can be used in two ways. The first way is to dissolve the powder in a small amount of water before stirring it into the frosting—this will ensure even and quick distribution through the frosting. Alternatively, they can be added directly to the frosting; however, mixing will take a little longer to prevent the frosting becoming streaked with small specks of concentrated color. Pastes are easily mixed straight into frosting a little at a time. Use the end of a small spoon or the tip of a knife to add pastes and powders. Never dip a moist or dirty skewer or knife into colors as this can ruin them.

liquids Liquids are generally the least concentrated but most readily available of the food colorings. Use a clean dropper or the tip of a clean skewer dipped in liquid colors and add gradually to achieve the desired color. Don't be afraid to mix colors to achieve the color you want. A color wheel or art book can help you know what colors to mix, otherwise experiment in a small bowl before adding to the frosting.

how to frost the cake

Once the frosting is tinted, it needs to be spread onto the cake. In most cases it is best to use a flat-bladed knife or palette knife for this purpose. However, you may find it easier to firstly pipe the frosting onto the smaller areas such as the eyes, or when many different-colored frostings are used. After you have piped the frosting onto the cake, spread it smooth with a palette knife. For a really smooth result, heat your knife in hot water and wipe it dry before dipping it in the frosting and smoothing it over. Repeat this process between each stroke.

Palette knives can be purchased at speciality kitchen shops and are available in various lengths and widths. It is good to have a small and a large palette knife for frosting different areas, but a good multi-purpose one has a 4-inch blade.

decoration

Once the cake is frosted, some cakes are nearly completed, but others need decorative touches such as candy and toys. All of these should be readily available from supermarkets, but you can easily improvise and use substitutes.

candy Candy is great for easy decorating as it comes in a huge range of colors, shapes, and sizes, and can be easily stuck onto the cake with a dab of leftover frosting. We have taken care to use candy and decorations that are readily available. Many supermarkets carry "pick and choose" candy selections where you can buy just a few of one type of candy instead of a whole package. Otherwise use the leftovers for children's candy bags. Speciality shops often sell a wide variety of more unusual and imported candies.

The candies we have used can usually be substituted with a similar-shaped candy or, if you are feeling creative, with others that you prefer. Candies to be trimmed or cut, such as licorice wheels or licorice straps, marshmallows, or jellybeans, may be cut with a sharp knife or scissors. To cut sticky candies such as marshmallows, dip the scissors or knife in confectioners' sugar or cornstarch before cutting so that the scissors don't stick together.

For safety reasons it is best to avoid hard candies and nuts on cakes for children under 3 years of age. Use soft candies or colored sprinkles instead to avoid choking.

other decorations Non-edible decorations used on our cakes have been bought from toy shops, supermarkets, craft shops, speciality shops, and department stores. These are not always absolutely necessary and can be substituted with similar items.

detailing

To mark the outline and highlights on cakes, we have used food gels, melted chocolate, piped frosting, and thin strips of licorice.

gels Edible gels come in a variety of different colors and are very easy to use as they can be squeezed straight from the tube.

melted chocolate To melt chocolate, chop the chocolate (or chocolate chips) and place in a heatproof bowl. Bring a saucepan of water to a boil and remove from the heat. Sit the bowl over the pan, making sure the base of the bowl is not touching the water. Stir occasionally, until the chocolate has melted. Alternatively, put the chocolate in a microwave-safe bowl and microwave on High in 30-second bursts, testing each time until melted.

piped frosting Sometimes we use leftover frosting to add the edging around cakes. For this, you need a piping bag. To make a piping bag, cut a 12-inch square of baking parchment in half diagonally. Twist the triangle into a cone shape (the center of the long side should end up being the tip of the piping bag). Fold the paper over at the other end to hold its shape. Fill the cone half to two-thirds full with frosting or melted chocolate, then seal by folding over the edges to keep the filling contained. Alternatively, you can use a small plastic bag: spoon the frosting or chocolate into the corner of a small, clean plastic bag, twist the top of the bag to secure, then snip the corner tip off the bag to pipe.

When piping, apply even pressure and make smooth movements to prevent the frosting clumping and breaking the line you are making. Hold the piping bag at a 45-degree angle when piping and squeeze gently from the top.

serving size

Generally a 1¼–1½ inch square piece of cake per child is sufficient for a children's party.

storing

To store a decorated cake, either lift the cake on its cake board into a container or, if the cake is too large, upturn a large box over the cake. Cakes can be stored for 2–3 days in a cool, dry place when frosted with buttercream. Meringue frosting should be stored at room temperature and eaten within 24 hours. Chocolate ganache frostings are best stored in a cool, dry place unless it is really hot, when refrigeration will be necessary; however, this can make the chocolate "sweat" and cause discoloring.

transporting cakes

If you have to move your party cake once it is decorated, place it in a clean covered box the same size as the cake board. If your box is too big, roll pieces of adhesive tape and put on the bottom of the cake board or straight into the bottom of the box to prevent the cake from sliding. Press firmly into the box to secure the cake. Put the boxed cake on a non-slip mat or sheet on a flat surface—on the floor or in the trunk of the car, not on the seat. Drive very carefully and take some leftover frosting, a spare piping bag, and a palette knife in case of touch-ups.

basic cake recipes

We used 11³/₄-ounce packages of butter cake mix to make our cakes. If you would prefer to make your own, the basic cake recipes here are equivalent to one package cake mix. Once the cake is cooled, wrap it in plastic wrap or place in an airtight container, then either store in a cool, dry place for up to 3 days or freeze for up to 3 months. If you are freezing your cake, thaw it for 2 hours before you start decorating.

butter cake

Preparation time: 25 minutes
Total cooking time: 45 minutes

²/₃ cup butter, softened
¹/₂ cup superfine sugar
2 eggs, lightly beaten
1¹/₂ teaspoons natural vanilla extract
1¹/₂ cups self-rising flour
¹/₃ cup milk

1 Preheat the oven to 350°F. Lightly grease a deep, 8-inch round cake pan and line the base with baking parchment.

2 Beat the butter and sugar with electric beaters until light and creamy. Add the eggs one at a time, beating well after each addition. Add the vanilla extract and beat until combined.

3 Using a large metal spoon, fold in the sifted flour alternately with the milk until smooth. Spoon the mixture into the pan and smooth the surface. Bake for 45 minutes, or until a skewer comes out clean when inserted into the center of the cake.

4 Leave the cake in the pan for at least 5 minutes before turning out onto a wire rack to cool completely.

chocolate cake

Preparation time: 25 minutes
Total cooking time: 45 minutes

²/₃ cup butter, softened
³/₄ cup superfine sugar
2 eggs, lightly beaten
1 teaspoon natural vanilla extract
1³/₄ cups self-rising flour
¹/₂ cup unsweetened cocoa powder
³/₄ cup milk

1 Preheat the oven to 350°F. Lightly grease a deep, 8-inch round cake pan and line the base with baking parchment.

2 Beat the butter and sugar in a large bowl with electric beaters until light and creamy. Add the eggs gradually, beating thoroughly after each addition. Add the vanilla extract and beat well.

3 Using a metal spoon, fold in the sifted flour and cocoa powder alternately with the milk. Stir until just smooth.

4 Spoon the mixture into the pan and smooth the surface. Bake for 45 minutes, or until a skewer comes out clean when inserted in the center. Leave the cake to cool in the pan for at least 5 minutes before turning out on a wire rack to cool completely.

the icing on the cake

Each of these frostings makes one quantity. If your cake needs more than one quantity of frosting, increase the ingredients proportionally. Each frosting will cover an 8-inch square or round cake.

buttercream

1 Beat the butter in a small bowl with electric beaters until pale and fluffy.

2 Continue beating and gradually add the vanilla extract and half the sifted confectioners' sugar.

3 Gradually add the milk and the remaining sugar and beat until smooth.

VARIATION: To make chocolate buttercream, mix 2 tablespoons of sifted unsweetened cocoa powder into the mixture.

**1/2 cup good-quality unsalted butter, at room temperature
1 teaspoon natural vanilla extract
1 1/2 cups confectioners' sugar
2 tablespoons milk, at room temperature**

meringue frosting

1 Stir the sugar and 1/3 cup water in a saucepan over low heat until the sugar has dissolved—do not allow to boil. Brush any sugar grains from the side of the pan with a pastry brush dipped in water. Increase the heat and boil without stirring for 3–5 minutes, or until the syrup reaches the soft ball stage (225°F on a sugar thermometer). Test by dropping a teaspoon of syrup into cold water—it will form a soft, sticky ball.

2 While the syrup is boiling, beat the egg whites with electric beaters in a small bowl until firm peaks form. When the syrup bubbles subside, gradually pour the syrup in a thin stream onto the egg whites, beating at medium speed. It will thicken and form stiff peaks.

**1 cup superfine sugar
2 egg whites**

white chocolate ganache

1 Put all the ingredients in a saucepan and stir over low heat until melted and smooth.

2 Transfer the mixture to a small bowl, cover the surface with plastic wrap and leave to cool completely. Do not refrigerate or it will go hard.

3 When cooled, beat with electric beaters for 8–10 minutes, or until thick, pale, and creamy.

**1 cup white chocolate chips
1 cup chopped white chocolate
1/2 cup whipping cream
1 cup unsalted butter, chopped**

enchanted
folk

enchanted village

CAKE AND EQUIPMENT

giant (1-cup) muffin pan
1/2 package cake mix (6 ounces)
four 6-inch jelly rolls
three 2-inch mini jelly rolls
14 x 14 inch cake board

DECORATION

2 1/2 quantities buttercream from
   page 11
food colorings: rose and violet
1 1/2 cups pink heart candies
1 cup white mints
9 ounces (about 25) pink candy sticks
assorted marshmallows
assorted pastel-colored candies

NOTE

Make sure you check the package size
of the cake mix before you start and
adjust the size accordingly.

1   Preheat the oven to 350°F. Lightly grease three cups of a giant muffin pan. Fill the cups three-quarters full with the cake mix, then bake for 20–25 minutes, or until cooked through. Cool in the pans, then loosen each muffin and turn out onto a wire rack to cool completely.

2   Cut one of the large jelly rolls in half. Cut one third off another of the large jelly rolls to create a large and a small roll. Trim the ends off all the rolls and mini jelly rolls so that they are level.

3   Cut the dome tops off the muffins, then turn over and trim the bottom of each muffin to resemble pointed roof tops.

4   Divide the buttercream equally between two bowls. Add a little rose coloring to one half and a little violet to the other half.

5   Stand lengths of the rolls on the cake board to form the buildings of the village, with the tallest rolls at the back. Once you are happy with the shape of your village, affix either a mini jelly roll or muffin to each building as a roof.

6   Frost the buildings and roofs with the two colors so that three are pink and three are purple, and affix to the cake board with a little extra buttercream. Finish the roofs by decorating one with heart candies, one with halved mints, one with thinly sliced pink candy sticks and the others with marshmallows—you may need a little extra buttercream to fasten the roof "tiles" in place.

7   To give the impression of brickwork, use a skewer to draw bricks into the walls of some of the buildings. Decorate the buildings with windows, doors, turrets, and other features made out of candies.

8   For the final touch, spread buttercream to make a couple of pathways leading away from the village, and sprinkle with assorted candies.

Trim the ends of the rolls; cut one in half and cut a third off another roll.

Cut the bottom of the muffins into the shape of a roof top.

Top the towers with muffin roof tops or mini jam rolls.

cuddly teddy bear

1 Preheat the oven to 350°F. Grease the cake pans and pudding mold and line the bases with parchment paper. Divide the cake mix evenly among the three pans and bake for 35–40 minutes, or until a skewer inserted into the center of the cakes comes out clean. Most ovens will fit all three cakes—make sure they are not touching; if they are, cook them separately. Cool in the pans for 5 minutes, then turn out onto a wire rack to cool completely.

2 Level the two round cakes, if necessary. Sit one of the cakes on the cake board and spread the top with buttercream. Sandwich the two cakes together. Trim a diagonal strip off the top and bottom edges of the cake sandwich to form a fat body. Sit the pudding-shaped cake on the body, with the flat side of the pudding on top. Push two skewers through the head and body to firmly secure them together. Trim any protruding skewer. Trim a diagonal slice around the bottom edge of the pudding to create a neck.

3 Cut a diagonal slice off the flat end of four mini jelly rolls and attach them to the body with skewers—two for the arms and two for the legs. Cut a ³/₄ inch slice off the remaining mini jelly roll and stick it onto the center of the face with a skewer—this is the snout. Make two slits on the top of the head where the ears should go, then push a cookie into each slit.

4 Tint ¹/₃ cup of the buttercream white. Add the cocoa to the remainder and beat well. Thickly spread the chocolate buttercream over the body, arms, and legs (reserve a tablespoon for piping). Frost the tummy, snout, and ears white. Rough up the buttercream with a palette knife so that it looks like fur.

5 To make the eyes, cut a marshmallow in half and stick a brown candy on each half with a dab of buttercream. Put the eyes in place. Use thin strips of licorice for the lips, a triangular piece for the nose, and a red jellybean for the mouth. Use a brown sugar-coated candy for a belly button. Using a piping bag filled with the reserved chocolate buttercream, pipe four small dots and one large dot on each chocolate chip for the paws, then press them gently in place.

CAKE AND EQUIPMENT
two 7-inch round cake pans
4-cup metal pudding mold
2 packages cake mix (23¹/₂ ounces)
12-inch round cake board
skewers
five 2-inch mini jelly rolls
ruler

DECORATION
1¹/₂ quantities buttercream from page 11
2 round chocolate cookies
¹/₄ cup unsweetened cocoa powder, sifted
1 white marshmallow
3 brown sugar-coated chocolate candies
licorice pieces
1 red jellybean
4 white chocolate chips

NOTE
Make sure you check the package size of the cake mix before you start and adjust the size accordingly.

Trim a diagonal slice around the top and bottom of the cakes to create a body.

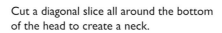

Cut a diagonal slice all around the bottom of the head to create a neck.

Secure the mini jelly rolls to the body with skewers.

marvin the martian

CAKE AND EQUIPMENT

8-inch round cake pan
1 package cake mix (11¾ ounces)
copy of template from page 126
toothpicks or skewers
12-inch round cake board

DECORATION

1 quantity buttercream from page 11
green food coloring
nonpareils
sugar-coated chocolate candies
cake decorating gels: red and blue
1 marshmallow
8 gumdrops
2 red lollipops

NOTE

Make sure you check the package size
of the cake mix before you start and
adjust the size accordingly.

1 Preheat the oven to 350°F. Grease the cake pan and line the base with parchment paper. Spoon the cake mix into the pan and bake for 35–40 minutes, or until a skewer inserted into the center of the cake comes out clean. Let the cake cool in the pan for 5 minutes before turning out onto a wire rack to cool completely.

2 Stick the crescent template onto the edge of the cake and secure it with skewers—if you think you will need help cutting out the neck, mark the neck marks onto the cake with a skewer or a toothpick. Cut out the crescent with a sharp knife. Remove the template and toothpicks, then cut the neck piece out from the middle of the crescent—keep the two side pieces for the ears.

3 Tint the buttercream bright green. Place the large piece of cake on the cake board and cover it with buttercream. Put the neck piece into position in the middle of the least curved side of the cake. Frost the neck with the buttercream.

4 Trim the domed top of the two ears so that they are level, then cover them with buttercream. Dip the ears into a saucer filled with nonpareils to coat them all over. Stick the ears into position on either side of the head, then attach a yellow sugar-coated chocolate candy to the tip of each with a little bit of buttercream.

5 Mark three ovals for the eyes onto the face with a toothpick or skewer, then fill the outlines with red gel. Cut the marshmallow into thirds and place one third on each oval. Top each one with a blue sugar-coated chocolate candy, securing with a little gel.

6 Use two red sugar-coated chocolate candies for the nostrils; put five gumdrops across the forehead, and three across the neck. Pipe a zigzag mouth with the blue gel and insert two lollipops into the top of the head for antennae.

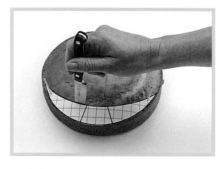

Stick the crescent template on the edge of the cake and cut the cake to shape.

Cut out the neck piece from the cake crescent.

Stick the neck piece into position in the middle of the flatter side of the head.

Roll the ears in nonpareils until well covered.

fairy princess

1   Remove the ice cream from the freezer for 15 minutes to soften a little. While you are waiting, make some space in the freezer wide enough to fit a 10-inch cake plate and tall enough to fit the pudding mold and the doll. Line the pudding mold with plastic wrap, with the ends overhanging the side. Transfer the ice cream to a large bowl and "mash" with a potato masher to help soften the ice cream, then spoon it into the lined pudding mold, smoothing the surface evenly. Cover the top of the ice cream with the overhanging plastic wrap and freeze for at least 4 hours, or until firm.

2   Take the pan out of the freezer and, working quickly, dip the base into warm water. Pull back the plastic wrap, put the cake plate over the pan and invert the ice cream onto the plate, then remove the mold and plastic wrap. Return the ice cream mound on its plate to the freezer for 1 hour, or until set.

3   Remove the ice cream from the freezer and, working quickly, use a teaspoon to scoop out enough ice cream from the top of the mound to sit the doll in up to her waist. Spoon back the ice cream around the doll to cement her into place. Tie the doll's hair back or cover it with plastic wrap to prevent her hair falling into the ice cream while decorating. Return to the freezer for 1 hour.

4   Put the cream and sugar in a bowl and begin whisking. Add a few drops of coloring at a time and whisk until firm peaks form. Remove the princess from the freezer. Using a spatula, cover the ice cream skirt with the whipped cream and shape into soft waves with a palette knife. Decorate the skirt with the silver dragées and sugared flowers, then return to the freezer for 1 hour, or until the cream is set.

5   Remove from the freezer. Wrap the dark ribbon around the body of the doll and seal at the back with adhesive tape. Wrap the sheer ribbon over the dark bodice and tie a big bow at the back to resemble wings. Groom the princess's hair and crown her with the tiara. Return to the freezer until ready to serve.

CAKE AND EQUIPMENT
16 cups ice cream
10-inch cake plate or board
8-cup pudding mold
small plastic doll with legs removed
adhesive tape

DECORATION
2½ cups heavy cream
1 tablespoon superfine sugar
yellow food coloring
silver dragées
yellow and pink sugared flowers
   (see Note)
8-inch length of solid pink ribbon
3-foot length of sheer ribbon
1 tiara

NOTE
We bought sugared flowers from a specialist cake decorating shop. You can also use material flowers available from fabric shops, but remember to remove them before serving.

Spoon the softened ice cream into the lined pudding mold.

Invert the frozen ice cream mound onto a cake plate.

Spoon ice cream back into the hole around the doll to cement her in place.

desmond the dinosaur

CAKE AND EQUIPMENT

9-inch square cake pan

8 x 12 inch rectangular cake pan

3 packages cake mix (35¼ ounces)

13 x 24 inch cake board

copy of template from page 127

toothpicks or skewers

DECORATION

2 quantities buttercream from page 11

food colorings: black and violet
  (we used powder)

2 mini white marshmallows

small and large green sugar-coated
  chocolate candies

NOTE

Make sure you check the package size
of the cake mix before you start and
adjust the size accordingly.

1 Preheat the oven to 350°F. Grease the cake pans and line the bases with parchment paper. Divide the cake mix evenly between the pans and bake the square cake for 45–50 minutes, then the rectangular cake for 25–30 minutes, or until a skewer inserted into the center of the cakes comes out clean. Let the cakes cool in the pans for 5 minutes before turning out onto a wire rack to cool completely.

2 Put about ¾ cup of the buttercream in a small bowl and tint it black. Tint the larger portion of the buttercream violet.

3 Arrange the cakes on the cake board as shown and secure with some buttercream. Position the template onto the cakes and secure with toothpicks. Cut the cakes to shape, then remove the template and toothpicks.

4 Spread violet buttercream over the whole cake, including the sides. Copying the template or picture, use a skewer or toothpick to draw the outlines and all the features onto the dinosaur—if you make a mistake, simply smooth it over and start again. Once you have the features marked out, contour the buttercream on the neck and legs with a palette knife, being careful not to erase your skewer marks. Pipe the outlines of the dinosaur with black buttercream, using your skewer marks as a guide.

5 Flatten the marshmallows slightly and put them into position for the eyes. Pipe a small dot on each marshmallow for the pupils. Arrange the candies randomly over the cake as shown.

Arrange the cakes on a cake board and stick together with a little buttercream.

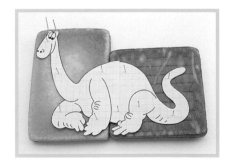

Stick the template onto the cake with the toothpicks.

Use a skewer or toothpick to trace the outline of the dinosaur's features.

Go over your skewer marks with the piping bag filled with black buttercream.

splash! mermaid

1 Preheat the oven to 350°F. Grease the cake pans and line the bases with parchment paper. Divide the cake mix evenly between the pans and bake (they should fit on the same shelf) for 25–30 minutes, or until a skewer inserted into the center of the cakes comes out clean. Let the cakes cool in the pans for 5 minutes before turning out onto a wire rack to cool completely.

2 Put the cakes on the cake board in a backward L shape, joining the edges with a little buttercream—level them so they are an even height. Position the template onto the cake and secure with toothpicks. Mark the bodice onto the cake by piercing through the paper with a skewer or toothpick. Using a small, sharp knife, cut the cake to shape. Remove the template and toothpicks.

3 Put half the buttercream in one bowl, then divide the remaining buttercream in half again and put each portion in a separate bowl. Tint the largest portion pale green, one portion blue, and the other portion pale peach. Frost the tail green, the bodice blue, and the head, neck, chest, and arms peach. Use a palette knife to give the buttercream on the tail a swirled texture.

4 Lightly sprinkle green sugar crystals over the tail. Decorate the bodice with dragées (we used silver, but you may prefer to decorate with a variety of colors), then make a necklace out of different colored dragées.

5 To make the hair, slice the apricot fruit leather into thin strips. Arrange the hair around the face and cascading over the shoulders. Pipe the mermaid's features onto her face with cake decorating gels: red for the mouth, black for the eyes and nose, and blue for the pupils.

CAKE AND EQUIPMENT
two 8 x 12 inch rectangular cake pans
3 packages cake mix (35 1/4 ounces)
12 x 20 inch cake board
copy of template from page 128
toothpicks or skewers

DECORATION
2 quantities buttercream from page 11
food colorings: green, blue, and peach
green sugar crystals (see Note)
assorted dragées
4 apricot fruit leather
cake decorating gels: red, black, and blue

NOTES
We bought ready-made colored sugar crystals, but you can make your own by placing sugar in a plastic bag and adding a drop or two of liquid food coloring. Close the bag and shake until the color disperses through the sugar.

Make sure you check the package size of the cake mix before you start and adjust the size accordingly.

Form the cakes into a backward L shape and stick the template in place.

Once you have frosted the mermaid, create swirls on the tail and bodice.

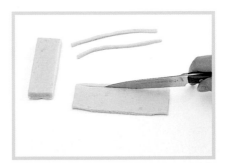

Use a sharp knife to cut very thin strips from the fruit roll-ups.

cranky witch

CAKE AND EQUIPMENT
two 6-cup round-based pudding molds
2 packages cake mix (23½ ounces)
12-inch square cake board
skewers
ruler

HAT
copy of template from page 129
cardboard
adhesive tape
stickers

DECORATION
2 quantities buttercream from page 11
food colorings: blue, peach, and black
   (we used powder for black)
1 ice cream cone
1 candy stick
two long licorice wheels or licorice
   straps
2 chocolate nonpareils
2 brown sugar-coated chocolate
   candies
black cake decorating gel

NOTE
Make sure you check the package size
of the cake mix before you start and
adjust the size accordingly.

1 Preheat the oven to 350°F. Grease the pudding molds and line the bases with parchment paper. Divide the cake mix evenly between the molds and bake for 40–45 minutes, or until a skewer comes out clean. Cool in the molds for 5 minutes before turning out onto a wire rack to cool completely.

2 Sit the cakes on top of each other and secure with two skewers. Trim the sides of the top cake to form the round head. Shave down the sides of the base cake at a 45-degree angle to form a body. Cut two triangles from the offcuts to create two arms.

3 Put three-quarters of the buttercream in a bowl and tint it blue. Put ½ cup of the remaining buttercream in another bowl and tint it pale peach. Tint the remaining buttercream black.

4 Frost the body blue and spread the peach buttercream over the face area. Stick the tip of the ice cream cone onto the middle of the face and frost it peach. Spread black buttercream over the back and top of the head.

5 Attach the arms to the body (you might need a skewer) and cover the sleeve with blue buttercream, but frost the hands peach. Attach the candy stick between the arms as a broom handle.

6 Cut six 5½-inch lengths and three 2-inch lengths of licorice. Cut into thin strips, but don't cut all the way through the strap (see picture).

7 Use the long lengths of licorice for the hair and use two of the shorter lengths as a fringe. Attach the final piece of licorice to the dress at the end of the candy stick for the broom head.

8 To make the spider, put two spots of frosting on the cake board and stick on two chocolate nonpareils and add legs of thin strips of licorice.

9 Use two brown candies for the eyes. Pipe the facial features with black gel so that the witch looks cranky. Add an extra two drops of blue food coloring to the remaining blue buttercream, transfer to a piping bag and pipe stripes at the front of the dress to make gathers.

10 Use the template to cut the cardboard into pieces for the hat. Roll the triangle into a cone and secure with tape or staples. Cut a small circle about 2 inches in diameter out of the center of the large circle to fit the cone into. Push the cone through the hole and secure with tape from the inside. Decorate with stickers, then put into place.

Shave off the sides of the bottom cake at a 45-degree angle.

Use one of the offcuts from the body to make two triangles for the arms.

Cut the licorice wheel into thin strips, but don't cut all the way through.

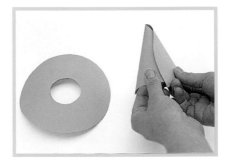

Cut out hat pieces from cardboard, then join together to form the hat.

CAKE AND EQUIPMENT

two 8¹/₂-inch round cake pans
3 packages cake mix (35¹/₄ ounces)
copy of template from page 130
toothpicks or skewers
11¹/₄ x 19 inch cake board
ruler

DECORATION

2 quantities buttercream from page 11
food colorings: blue, yellow, and green
1 long licorice wheel or licorice strap
2 large red gum balls
cake decorating gels: red and black
3 blue sugar-coated chocolate candies
2 white marshmallows
rainbow and red fruit roll-ups

NOTE

Make sure you check the package size
of the cake mix before you start and
adjust the size accordingly.

1 Preheat the oven to 350°F. Grease the cake pans and line the bases with parchment paper. Divide the cake mix evenly between the pans and bake for 45–50 minutes, or until a skewer inserted into the center of the cakes comes out clean. Cool the cakes in the pans for 5 minutes before turning out onto a wire rack to cool completely.

2 Level the cakes if necessary, then turn them over. Secure the hat template to one cake and cut to shape. Pierce the paper with a skewer or toothpick to mark the lines between the stripes. Remove the template and toothpicks. Cut a 1¼-inch slice off the top of the other cake, leaving a straight edge. Piece the clown together on the cake board and join the pieces with buttercream.

3 Divide the buttercream in half and leave one half white, then divide the remaining mixture into thirds and tint one part blue, one part yellow, and the other part green. Frost the face with the white buttercream and the hat in alternating stripes of blue and yellow. Lastly, frost the bow tie with the green buttercream.

4 Cut the licorice wheel into thin strips, then into the following lengths: 1½ inches, 3¼ inches, 4½ inches, 6½ inches, and two 8 inches for the hat; two 2¾ inches, four 3¼ inches, two 4¼ inches, and two 4½ inches for the bow tie. Outline the hat and bow tie with these strips.

5 Stick one of the gum balls on the tip of the hat and the other one in the center of the face. Use a skewer to mark the outline of the eyes, then go over your markings with red gel. Next, use two blue candies stuck onto two marshmallows for the center of the eyes. Use another blue candy for the center of the bow tie.

6 Slightly stretch out a red fruit roll-up and, using scissors, cut out a smiley mouth and two small round dots for the cheeks—you can either use the template or do it freehand. Press gently into place. With the black gel, fill in the outline of the mouth and add the eyelashes.

7 Just before serving, make the hair: slice the rainbow fruit straps into thin strips and twirl around a pencil to create curls. Put the hair around the face.

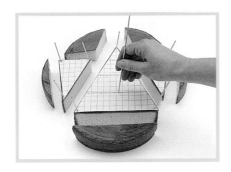

Cut out the cake pieces, then mark the stripes by piercing the cake.

Join the hat to the round cake and make a bow tie out of the small pieces.

Twist strips of fruit roll-up around a pencil or pen to make curls.

ferocious monster

CAKE AND EQUIPMENT

two 8 x 12 inch rectangular cake pans
3 packages cake mix (35¼ ounces)
10 x 14 inch cake board
copy of template from page 131
toothpicks or skewers

DECORATION

2 quantities buttercream from page 11
food colorings: green and black
  (we used powder for black)
licorice allsorts (striped licorice
  candies)
1 long licorice wheel or licorice strap
red cake decorating gel or strawberry
  sauce

NOTE

Make sure you check the package size
of the cake mix before you start and
adjust the size accordingly.

1   Preheat the oven to 350°F. Grease the cake pans and line the bases with parchment paper. Divide the cake mix evenly between the pans and bake for 25–30 minutes, or until a skewer inserted into the center of the cakes comes out clean. Let the cakes cool in the pans for 5 minutes before turning out onto a wire rack to cool completely.

2   Put the cakes on the cake board and join them along the long edges with a little buttercream. Cut out the pieces of the template and position onto the cakes as shown, securing with a few toothpicks. Cut the cakes to shape with a small, sharp knife. Use a skewer or toothpick to mark out the mouth and the basic shape of the hair area by piercing through the paper onto the cake. Remove the templates and toothpicks.

3   Cut the eyes in half so that they are half their original height. Shave off one long side of the brow at a 45-degree angle to form the jutting forehead.

4   Tint three-quarters of the buttercream green. Tint the remainder of the buttercream black. Frost the marked-out hair and mouth sections black, reserving 2 tablespoons of the black buttercream for the outline. Frost the entire face green. Position the forehead, eyes, and nose on the face, then frost them green.

5   Trim nine pieces of yellow fondant from the licorice allsorts for the teeth. Put them in position, trimming those at the edges so that they fit the mouth.

6   Cut the licorice wheel into varying lengths and thicknesses to create stringy hair and lay over the black buttercream—don't worry about being neat. Put the reserved black buttercream in a small piping bag and pipe on all the features. Use red gel to pipe the blood dripping from the mouth.

Stick the template onto the cake and mark
the mouth and hair with a skewer.

Cut the eyes in half, then shave a
45-degree angle off the brow.

Once the face is frosted, put the nose,
eyes, and forehead into position.

wonder
world

creepy-crawly caterpillar

CAKE AND EQUIPMENT

six ³/₄-cup small pie pans
1 package cake mix (11³/₄ ounces)
copy of template from page 132
ruler
12 x 22 inch cake board

DECORATION

¹/₂ quantity white chocolate ganache
  from page 11
assorted sprinkles
3 fruit rings
1 long licorice wheel or licorice strap

NOTE

Make sure you check the package size
of the cake mix before you start and
adjust the size accordingly.

1 Preheat the oven to 375°F. Grease the pie pans. Line the bases with small
   rounds of non-stick parchment paper. Divide the cake mix among the pie pans
   and bake for 15–20 minutes, or until a skewer comes out clean when inserted
   into the center of the cakes. Leave in the pans for 5 minutes, then turn out
   onto a wire rack to cool completely.

2 Using the template, cut a small crescent from one side of five of the cakes, so
   they fit snugly together. These five cakes are the body pieces; the remaining
   round cake will be the head.

3 Spread the top of each cake with the white chocolate ganache. Cover
   two-thirds of a cake with the template and decorate the exposed area with
   sprinkles. Move the template over so that more of the cake is exposed and
   sprinkle this crescent with different colored sprinkles. Remove the template
   and sprinkle the final area with a third color. Repeat with the other cakes, using
   alternating colored sprinkles.

4   Cover the head cake all over with chocolate sprinkles. Choose two pink fruit rings that are a good round shape for the eyes, and another to cut in half for the mouth. Cut the licorice wheel into thin strips, then cut two small pieces of licorice to fit in the eye rings. Gently scrape some of the sprinkles away from the eye and mouth areas, and press the features into place. Cut ten 1 1/2-inch lengths of licorice for the legs and two 2-inch lengths for the antennae.

5   Arrange the caterpillar on the cake board, making the body pieces alternately slightly higher and lower, so it looks like it is wriggling. Join the pieces with a little ganache. Attach the legs and antennae by pushing them into the cake; they will rest slightly on the board.

Use the template to help you make colored stripes on the body pieces.

Stick the eyes and mouth on the face in the areas cleared of sprinkles.

Stick the antennae and legs into the sides of the cake and rest them on the board.

fresh as a daisy

1. Preheat the oven to 350°F. Grease the loaf pans and line the bases with parchment paper. Divide the cake mix evenly between the pans and bake for 35–40 minutes, or until a skewer inserted into the center of the cakes comes out clean. Cool the cakes in the pans for 5 minutes before turning out onto a wire rack to cool completely.

2. Level the cakes if necessary. Position the flower template on the round cake and the leaf template on the long cake and secure with toothpicks. Cut the cakes to shape. Remove the template and toothpicks.

3. Stick one chocolate bar on top of another with a little buttercream. Repeat with the other two chocolate bars to make the stem. Sit the flower cake on the cake board, add the chocolate stem underneath the flower and position the leaves on either side of the stem.

4. Put one-third of the buttercream in a bowl and tint it green, then tint the larger portion light orange. Spread the orange buttercream all over the flower, making shallow furrows in the petals with a palette knife. Put the cookie cutter in the center of the cake and pour orange sprinkles in the middle of it. Carefully lift off the cookie cutter.

5. Frost the leaves with the green buttercream. Cut the fruit leaves in half horizontally and overlap on the cake leaves. Sit the butterfly on the flower.

CAKE AND EQUIPMENT
8½-inch round cake pan
10 x 3 x 5 inch loaf pan
2 packages cake mix (23½ ounces)
copy of template from page 133
toothpicks
12 x 20 inch cake board
small round cookie cutter

DECORATION
4 flaked chocolate bars
2 quantities buttercream from page 11
food colorings: green and orange
orange sprinkles
candied fruit leaves
toy butterfly

NOTE
Make sure you check the package size of the cake mix before you start and adjust the size accordingly.

Put all the cake pieces into position, using the chocolate bar as the stem.

Sit the candied fruit leaves on the cake leaves, slightly overlapping each other.

Once the flower has been frosted, make furrows with a palette knife.

hopping rabbit

CAKE AND EQUIPMENT

two 8 x 12 inch rectangular cake pans
2 packages cake mix (23½ ounces)
copy of template from pages 134–135
toothpicks
16-inch square cake board

DECORATION

1 quantity white chocolate ganache
    from page 11
food colorings: orange and pink
1 candied fruit leaf
1 pink marshmallow
¼ cup white chocolate chips
1 pink sugar-coated chocolate candy
5 mini mints

NOTE

Make sure you check the package size
of the cake mix before you start and
adjust the size accordingly.

1 Preheat the oven to 350°F. Grease the cake pans and line the bases with parchment paper. Divide the cake mix evenly between the pans and bake for 20–25 minutes, or until a skewer inserted into the center of the cakes comes out clean. Let the cakes cool in the pans for 5 minutes before turning out onto a wire rack to cool completely.

2 Cut out the body pieces from the template, position on the cakes and secure each piece with a toothpick. Cut the cakes to shape, then remove the template and toothpicks. Slice the leg piece in half lengthwise so that it is half the thickness of the other pieces. Discard one half of the leg. Assemble the cake on the cake board as shown, joining the pieces with a little ganache.

3 Tint 2 tablespoons of the ganache bright orange. Tint the remainder pale pink. Transfer 2 tablespoons of the pink ganache to a small bowl and tint it darker pink for the ears and tail. Cover the cake with a thick layer of the pale pink ganache, leaving the tail and center of the ears unfrosted. Make soft waves in the ganache with a palette knife. Frost the centers of the ears and the tail with the darker-pink ganache.

4 Put the carrot on the cake board in front of the rabbit and frost it with orange ganache. Make cuts in the candied fruit leaf three-quarters of the way through to resemble the leafy top of a carrot. Attach to the top of the carrot.

5 Slice the marshmallow in half horizontally and stick half in place for the nose. Put the chocolate chips in a heatproof bowl. Bring a saucepan of water to the boil, then remove from the heat. Sit the bowl over the pan, making sure the base of the bowl does not touch the water. Stir occasionally until the chocolate has melted. Pipe eight chocolate lines of various lengths on a tray lined with parchment paper—you will only need four, but it is good to have extra. Leave the whiskers for 5–10 minutes to set. Then, stick the four whiskers in place. Give the rabbit an eye using a pink sugar-coated chocolate candy. Use one mini mint for a buck tooth, and another four for claws. Draw on the mouth with a skewer.

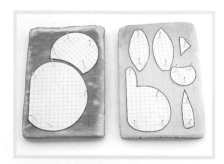

Stick all the template pieces into position on the two cakes.

Piece the rabbit together, then join all the pieces with a little ganache.

Pipe eight thin lengths of melted chocolate onto a tray covered with parchment paper.

volcano vesuvius

1. In a large bowl, combine 7 cups of the puffed rice cereal and 1/2 cup of the coconut, then sift in 1/2 cup of the cocoa powder and 1 3/4 cups of the confectioners' sugar. Mix together and make a well in the center. Melt 12 ounces of the vegetable shortening in a saucepan over low heat. Pour into the well and mix together. Spoon the mixture into the pudding mold and refrigerate for 4 hours, or until hard and set. Turn out the chocolate mixture onto the cake board.

2. Make the same quantity of chocolate mixture again and cool completely. Once cool, use the extra mixture to build up the shape of the volcano, molding with your hands. Supporting the top of the volcano with one hand, scoop out a hollow in the top of the volcano with a spoon—this will be the crater. Put the volcano in the refrigerator to set.

3. Put the chocolate in a heatproof bowl. Bring a saucepan of water to the boil, then remove from the heat. Sit the bowl over the pan, making sure the base of the bowl does not sit in the water. Stir occasionally until the chocolate has melted. Cut long strips of fruit roll-ups, narrower at the top and wider at the bottom, to represent flowing lava. Stick them to the sides of the volcano—you shouldn't need to use anything to stick them on, but if you are transporting the cake, use a little melted chocolate. Drizzle some of the melted chocolate down the sides of the volcano. Stick chunks of rocky road, honeycomb, and chocolate onto the volcano with a dab of melted chocolate so that they will stay in place. Just before serving, scrunch up some cellophane and stick it into the crater to look like billowing flames.

CAKE AND EQUIPMENT

14 cups puffed rice cereal
1 cup dried coconut
1 cup unsweetened cocoa powder
3 1/2 cups confectioners' sugar
3 cups white vegetable shortening
8-cup pudding mold
14-inch square cake board

DECORATION

1 cup chopped dark chocolate
red and orange fruit roll-ups
3/4 cup broken rocky road
3 1/2 ounces honeycomb
3 1/2 ounces chocolate bar with triangular pieces, broken
red and yellow cellophane

NOTE

If you are going to transport this cake, put the finished cake in the refrigerator for at least 30 minutes before traveling so that the chocolate mixture is nice and hard. If it is a hot day, take a bottle of self-hardening chocolate sauce to stick on any "rocks" that might fall off.

Spoon the chocolate mixture into the pudding basin.

Build up the shape of the volcano with the extra chocolate mixture.

Stick the pieces of honeycomb onto the volcano, securing with melted chocolate.

little miss ladybird

CAKE AND EQUIPMENT
9½-inch round cake pan
2 packages cake mix (23½ ounces)
14-inch square cake board
copy of template from page 136
toothpicks
ruler

DECORATION
1½ quantities buttercream from page 11
food colorings: light brown and red
1 long licorice wheel or licorice strap
giant sugar-coated chocolate candies

NOTES
We have been creative with our ladybird; if you want her to be more realistic, use black candies for the spots and create only three sets of legs.

Make sure you check the package size of the cake mix before you start and adjust the size accordingly.

1 Preheat the oven to 350°F. Grease the cake pan and line with parchment paper. Pour the cake mix into the pan and bake for 35–40 minutes, or until a skewer inserted into the center of the cake comes out clean. Let the cake cool in the pan for 5 minutes before turning out onto a wire rack to cool completely.

2 Sit the cake on the cake board, position the template of the body on the cake and secure with toothpicks. Cut the cake to shape. Remove the template and toothpicks. Turn one of the offcuts on its side, put the head template on it and cut to shape. Repeat with the other offcut so that you have two bits of head. Put the two head sections on top of each other, sticking them together with a little buttercream.

3 To shape the body into a dome, shave all around the cake with a large serrated knife, as shown. Position the cake on the cake board and attach the head to the body with a little buttercream. Use a small, sharp knife to round the top of the head.

4 Reserve 2 tablespoons of the buttercream and tint it caramel brown. Tint the remainder of the buttercream bright red and frost the body with it. Next, frost the head with the brown buttercream.

5 Cut a 10¾-inch long piece of licorice and split the bottom third of the strip into two thin strips. Lay the licorice strip along the center of the body with the split at the tail end—this is the wing parting. Cut the remaining licorice into thin strips and cut about 12 very short pieces, about ½–¾ inches from the strip, to make the eyes. Next, cut eight 2-inch lengths out of the licorice strips for the legs. Stick the eyes and legs in place.

6 Dot giant sugar-coated chocolate candies all over the body and cut one of the red candies in half for the mouth—if they don't stick to the frosting, dab the bottom of them with a little extra buttercream.

Turn the offcut onto its side and cut around the head template with a knife.

Once the head is in position, round out the top with a small, sharp knife.

Using a palette knife, frost the head with the light brown buttercream.

Split the bottom third of the licorice wheel in two.

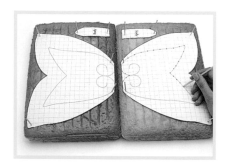

Use a skewer to transfer the wing pattern onto the cake.

Join the butterfly pieces together with some buttercream.

Sprinkle the center of the wing with the rainbow choc chips.

beautiful butterfly

1 Preheat the oven to 350°F. Grease the cake pans and line the bases with parchment paper. Divide the cake mix evenly between the pans and bake for 25–30 minutes, or until a skewer inserted into the center of the cakes comes out clean. Let the cakes cool in the pans for 5 minutes before turning out onto a wire rack to cool completely.

2 Sit the cakes on the cake board, put the template pieces into position and secure with toothpicks. Use a skewer or toothpick to mark the wing pattern onto the cake by piercing through the paper.

3 Cut out the body pieces, then the wings. Remove the template and toothpicks. Move the pieces together into the shape of a butterfly and join with a little buttercream.

4 Leave half the buttercream white and tint the remaining buttercream with a few drops of red food coloring. Frost the body and the center section of the wings with the white buttercream. Cut the licorice into thin strips and outline the wing pattern. Cover the center of the wings with the rainbow choc chips.

5 Spread pink buttercream over the rest of the butterfly and make slight furrows in the pink buttercream with a palette knife.

6 Decorate the edge of the butterfly's wings with mini gumdrops. Use two dark gumdrops for the eyes. Put the chocolate chips in a heatproof bowl. Bring a saucepan of water to the boil, then remove from the heat. Sit the bowl over the pan, making sure the base of the bowl does not sit in the water. Stir occasionally until the chocolate has melted. Spoon the chocolate into a piping bag. Pipe two feelers onto a sheet of parchment paper, allow to set, then stick into the top of the body, just underneath the eyes.

CAKE AND EQUIPMENT
two 8 x 12 inch rectangular cake pans
3 packages cake mix (35¼ ounces)
14 x 18 inch cake board
2 copies of template from page 137
toothpicks or skewers

DECORATION
1½ quantities buttercream from page 11
red food coloring
1 long licorice wheel or licorice strap
¾ cup rainbow choc chips
mini gumdrops
¼ cup dark chocolate chips

NOTE
Make sure you check the package size of the cake mix before you start and adjust the size accordingly.

tropical fish

CAKE AND EQUIPMENT
two 8½-inch round cake pans
2 packages cake mix (23½ ounces)
copy of template from page 138
toothpicks or skewers
16 x 22 inch cake board

DECORATION
1½ quantities buttercream from page 11
food colorings: red and blue
blue and purple sprinkles
3–4 licorice ropes
red cake decorating gel
1 round mint
sugar-coated chocolate candies
rainbow choc chips

NOTE
Make sure you check the package size
of the cake mix before you start and
adjust the size accordingly.

1 Preheat the oven to 350°F. Grease the cake pans
and line the bases with parchment paper. Divide the
cake mix evenly between the pans and bake for
25–30 minutes, or until a skewer inserted into the
center of the cakes comes out clean. Let the cakes cool
in the pans for 5 minutes before turning out onto a
wire rack to cool completely.

2 Level the cakes if necessary. Position the body template on
one cake and secure with toothpicks. Mark the stripes onto
the cake by piercing through the paper with a skewer or
toothpick. Using a small, sharp knife, cut out the mouth.
Remove the template and toothpicks. Cut out the other pieces
of the template and place on the other cake as shown, then secure with
toothpicks. Cut out the pieces.

3 Assemble the fish on the cake board as shown, rounding out the fins if
they need it so that they join the body neatly.

4 Put half the buttercream in one bowl, and a quarter each into two smaller
bowls. Tint the larger portion pink, tint one-quarter blue and leave the rest
of the buttercream white.

5 Spread the white buttercream onto the face. Frost the middle stripe, tail
and the air bubbles with the blue buttercream. Attach the fins to the cake
by butting them against the blue stripe. Frost the first and third stripes and
the fins with the pink buttercream.

6 Fill one saucer with blue sprinkles and one with purple sprinkles
and dip an air bubble into each until they are well coated.

7 Outline the stripes and accent the tail with licorice ropes. Pipe around the
edge of the mouth with red gel. Create an eye with the mint and a chocolate
candy: use a dab of any leftover buttercream to stick them together, and put
into place. Decorate the fish's stripes with the sugar-coated chocolate candies.
To finish, sprinkle rainbow choc chips on the tips of the tail.

Mark the stripes onto the cake by piercing
through the template with a skewer.

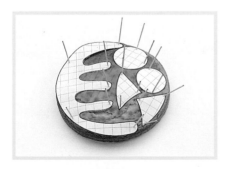

Put the other template pieces on the second cake and secure with toothpicks.

Make the shape of the fish with the pieces of cake.

Outline the fish's mouth with red cake decorating gel.

Return the cake to the roasting pan, sitting it over the set jelly.

Carefully pull the foil off the jelly, but don't worry if a little jelly sticks to the foil.

Spread the buttercream around the sides of the cake.

reef-world aquarium

1 Preheat the oven to 350°F. Grease the pan and line the base with parchment paper. Pour the cake mix into the pan and bake for 40–45 minutes, or until a skewer inserted into the center of the cake comes out clean. Let the cake cool in the pan for 5 minutes before turning out onto a wire rack to cool completely. Once cool, cover the cake in plastic wrap.

2 Clean the roasting pan and line it with foil; lightly oil the foil. Make up the blue jello according to the package instructions and pour into the pan. Refrigerate for about 6 hours, or until set.

3 Lay the crackers out on a work surface and use a pastry brush to dust off any flavoring powder. Turn the sharks over so the white side is facing up and trim the blue side so that they will sit flat. Paint the crackers with food coloring and draw patterns on the sharks with a toothpick dipped in coloring.

4 Using a sharp knife, cut the gummi snake into pieces about 2³⁄₄ inches long try to get two colors on each piece. Holding one end of each length, make two splits in the other end. Fan out the cut sections to resemble coral or seaweed.

5 Unwrap the cake, level it if necessary and take the jello out of the refrigerator. Put the cake, bottom-side-down, on the jello. Hold the cake board over the cake and carefully invert the pan so that the cake is on the bottom and the jello turns out onto the cake. Carefully peel back the foil—use a small knife to ease the jello from the foil around the edges, if necessary.

6 Tint the buttercream with a few drops of the blue food coloring and spread it around the sides of the cake, coming right up the sides of the jello. Swirl the buttercream with a palette knife so that it looks like swirling water.

7 Sprinkle the rainbow choc chips along the bottom of the jello. Cut the shell chocolates in half along the seam, and add to the cake. Put the coral in place, then arrange the fish. Refrigerate until required (don't cover); the cake will keep for up to 18 hours in the refrigerator.

CAKE AND EQUIPMENT
8 x 12 x 2 inch roasting pan
2 packages cake mix (23¹⁄₂ ounces)
two 3-ounce boxes of blue jello
1 pastry brush or small paintbrush
toothpicks
12 x 16 inch cake board

DECORATION
fish-shaped crackers
3 candy sharks
food colorings: red, blue, and yellow
1 giant multi-colored gummi snake or different colored gummi snakes
¹⁄₂ quantity buttercream from page 11
rainbow choc chips
2–4 chocolate shells, at room temperature (see Note)

NOTES
Because the chocolates get cut along the seam, you only need two chocolates, but we used four for extra variety.

Make sure you check the package size of the cake mix before you start and adjust the size accordingly.

spotty the dog

CAKE AND EQUIPMENT

7¹/₂-inch square cake pan
8¹/₂-inch round cake pan
2 packages cake mix (23¹/₂ ounces)
copy of template from page 139
toothpicks
12 x 18 inch cake board

DECORATION

2 quantities buttercream from page 11
2 tablespoons unsweetened cocoa
   powder, sifted
³/₄ cup grated dark chocolate
1 chocolate-coated cookie
white and pink marshmallows
sugar-coated chocolate candies
1 long licorice wheel or licorice strap
small dog collar (see Note)

NOTES

We have used a real collar, but if
you want to make a candy collar, place
a piece of licorice wheel under the
dog's chin and secure sugar-coated
chocolate candies to it with a little
buttercream.

Make sure you check the package size
of the cake mix before you start and
adjust the size accordingly.

1   Preheat the oven to 350°F. Grease the cake pans and line the bases with parchment paper. Divide the cake mix evenly between the pans and bake the square cake for 35–40 minutes, then the round cake for 35–40 minutes, or until a skewer inserted into the center of the cakes comes out clean. Let the cakes cool in the pans for 5 minutes before turning out onto a wire rack to cool completely.

2   Level the cakes if necessary. Cut out the templates of the ears and stick on the square cake with toothpicks. Cut out the head template and secure it to the round cake. Cut the cakes to shape, then remove the templates and toothpicks. Transfer the cake to the cake board, push the ears against the head and attach them with a little buttercream.

3   Put one-third of the buttercream into a bowl, add the cocoa and beat well. Use the remaining white buttercream to spread over the dog's face and ears, leaving odd-shaped gaps here and there—these will be filled with chocolate buttercream to represent the spots.

4   Use the chocolate buttercream to fill in the unfrosted gaps. Smooth the buttercream on the face and rough up the buttercream on the ears with a knife. Gently press the grated chocolate onto the spots.

5   Stick the chocolate cookie in the middle of the face for the nose. To make the eyes, cut a white marshmallow in half and stick a blue sugar-coated chocolate candy onto each half with a little buttercream. Stick the eyes just above the nose. Trim the rounded end off a halved pink marshmallow for the tongue and put it slightly below the nose. Cut the licorice into thin strips, then cut three short lengths of licorice for the eyebrows and tongue and two longer pieces for the snout. Place them into position, then snip tiny pieces of licorice for the spots around the nose and sprinkle them onto the cake. Add a red sugar-coated chocolate candy at the top of the tongue. Sit the collar below the head.

Sit the cake on a board and join the ears to the head with some buttercream.

Spread the white buttercream over the dog, leaving gaps for the chocolate spots.

To make a candy collar, add a strip of licorice with candies stuck to it.

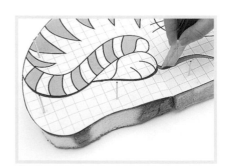

Separate the mat from the cake by cutting the cake along the split section.

Spread violet buttercream over the mat with a palette knife.

Fill in the cat's stripes by piping dark orange buttercream into them.

cat on a mat

1   Preheat the oven to 350°F. Grease the cake pans and line the bases with parchment paper. Divide the mixture evenly between the pans and bake for 45–50 minutes, or until a skewer inserted into the center of the cakes comes out clean. Let the cakes cool in the pans for 5 minutes before turning out onto a wire rack to cool completely.

2   Set aside ¹/₂ cup of the buttercream for the white areas. Tint 1 cup of the buttercream violet for the mat and tint the remainder pale orange (using a combination of red and yellow) for the body. Get two smaller bowls and put ¹/₄ cup of the orange buttercream in one bowl and ¾ cup in another. Tint the smaller portion medium orange and the larger portion dark orange.

3   Level the top of the cakes, then place them on the cake board, joining the edges with a little buttercream. Cut out the template, then cut along the line which separates the cat's body from the mat. Position the two pieces of template on the cake and secure with toothpicks. Cut around the edge of the template, then cut along the edge of the mat so that the cake is in two pieces—this will make the frosting easier to do. Remove the templates and toothpicks.

4   Spread the violet buttercream over the mat. Spread the pale orange buttercream all over the cat's body, then join the two pieces of cake together with some of the buttercream.

5   Using the template as a reference, mark all the cat's stripes onto the frosting with a skewer or toothpick. Transfer the darkest orange buttercream to a piping bag and fill in the dark orange stripes, using your skewer marks as a guide. Smooth the buttercream with a small palette knife.

6   Spread white buttercream in the ear areas, mouth area, and tips of the tail and paws, and blend softly into the pale orange buttercream so that you don't end up with sharp lines. Draw all the cat's remaining features onto the frosting with a skewer—these will help you with the piping.

7   Put the medium-colored orange buttercream into a small piping bag and pipe over your skewer marks to outline the cat's body, head, tail, claws, and around the stripes—but don't do the features that will be marked in chocolate.

8   Put a jellybean in position for the nose. Melt the chocolate as described on page 9, spoon into a piping bag and pipe the eyes, mouth, and paws with melted chocolate, following the skewer marks. Pipe whiskers onto a sheet of parchment paper. When set, lift into place. Drop silver dragées around the whiskers.

CAKE AND EQUIPMENT
two 9-inch square cake pans
3 packages cake mix (35¹/₄ ounces)
10 x 16 inch cake board
copy of template from page 140
toothpicks or skewers

DECORATION
2¹/₂ quantities buttercream from page 11
food colorings: violet, red, and yellow
1 red jellybean
¹/₃ cup dark chocolate chips
silver dragées

NOTE
Make sure you check the package size of the cake mix before you start and adjust the size accordingly.

fatty the whale

CAKE AND EQUIPMENT

two 8 x 12-inch rectangular cake pans
3 packages cake mix (35¼ ounces)
20-inch square cake board
copy of template from page 141
toothpicks or skewers

DECORATION

1½ quantities meringue frosting
   from page 11
food colorings: blue and red
1 long licorice wheel or licorice strap
marshmallows
1 blue sugar-coated chocolate candy
egg white
blue and green sprinkles

NOTE

Make sure you check the package size
of the cake mix before you start and
adjust the size accordingly.

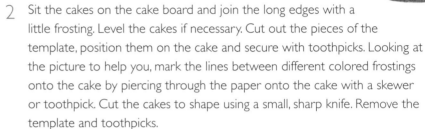

1 Preheat the oven to 350°F. Grease the cake pans and line the
bases with parchment paper. Divide the cake mix evenly between
the pans and bake for 20–25 minutes, or until a
skewer inserted into the center of the cakes
comes out clean. Let the cakes cool in the pans
for 5 minutes before turning out onto a wire rack
to cool completely.

2 Sit the cakes on the cake board and join the long edges with a
little frosting. Level the cakes if necessary. Cut out the pieces of the
template, position them on the cake and secure with toothpicks. Looking at
the picture to help you, mark the lines between different colored frostings
onto the cake by piercing through the paper onto the cake with a skewer
or toothpick. Cut the cakes to shape using a small, sharp knife. Remove the
template and toothpicks.

3 Put the whale on the cake board, move the fins and waterspout into place
and attach with a little frosting.

4 Reserve one-third of the meringue frosting and tint the remaining frosting blue.
Spread the blue frosting over the areas you have marked out with the skewer,
leaving the undercarriage, mouth, spot, and spout unfrosted.

5 Take 2 tablespoons of the remaining white meringue frosting, add a drop of
red coloring and use this pink frosting to fill in the mouth. Use the remaining
white frosting to frost the undercarriage of the whale, the spot, and the spout,
peaking the frosting on the spout to represent water.

6 Cut the licorice into long, thin strips. Outline the blue part of the whale
and the mouth with licorice strips. Cut a marshmallow in half and stick a blue
sugar-coated chocolate candy on top (securing it with a little frosting) and put
it in place for the eye. Add a small strip of licorice for the eyebrow. To make air
bubbles, dip marshmallows in egg white and coat with sprinkles.

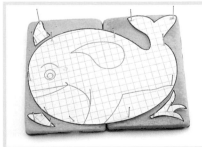

Position the template pieces on the joined cakes and secure with toothpicks.

Place the cake pieces into position and join with a little of the frosting.

Spread the frosting over the body of the whale with a palette knife.

mini cakes

Pick your four favorite mini cake designs and make six of each. Preheat the oven to 350°F. Use one package of cake mix (11¾ ounces) and fill two 12-cup standard muffin pans two-thirds full. Bake for 20 minutes, or until a skewer inserted into the center comes out clean. Cool, then decorate. You will need a half-quantity of buttercream (see page 11) to frost 24 mini cakes.

lovely ladybird

Tint 2 tablespoons of the buttercream pale pink with 1 drop of red food coloring. Spread onto the cakes. Put a chocolate chip in the center of the cake. Using imitation chocolate cake decorating gel, pipe the spots, face, head, and wing parting onto the ladybird. Make legs out of thin strips of licorice. Decorate the cake with silver dragées. Makes 6.

frog in a pond

Tint 2 tablespoons of buttercream with 4–5 drops of blue food coloring. Spread onto the cakes. Tint 1 tablespoon dried coconut with 1 drop of green coloring and add to one side. Sit a frog on top. Makes 6.

purring pussycat

Tint 2 tablespoons of buttercream orange with 2 drops of yellow and 1 drop of red food coloring. Use a pink candy to make the nose. Position the nose and make whiskers from banana candies. Draw the mouth with imitation chocolate cake decorating gel. Halve a green sugar-coated chocolate candy and position on the cake for the eyes. Snip a pink marshmallow in half and position on the cake for the ears. Pinch the tops to make pointy ears. Makes 6.

flower power

Lightly whisk 1 egg white. Using a paintbrush, paint nonsprayed rose petals with a little egg white. Sprinkle with superfine sugar. Sit on a wire rack to set (about 30 minutes). Spread 2 tablespoons of buttercream over the cakes and top with sugared petals. Line the edges of the cake with dragées. Makes 6.

well-dressed bear

Spread 2 tablespoons of chocolate buttercream over the cakes. Halve 1 brown sugar-coated chocolate candy and position, cut-side-up, for the eyes. Cut a black jellybean in half for the nose. Trim a piece of licorice to form the mouth, and larger pieces for the ears. Use an orange candy to make the bow tie. Makes 6.

swinging cherries

Tint 2 tablespoons of buttercream pale pink with 1–2 drops of red food coloring. Cut glacé cherries in half. Cut candied fruit leaves in half lengthwise and trim to make small leaves. Frost the cakes, position the cherries and make stems by cutting thin pieces of licorice. Press the leaves on. Makes 6.

prickly porcupine

Spread the cakes with chocolate buttercream. Arrange small strips of licorice for the spikes. Cut black jellybeans in half and stick, round-side-up, for the eyes. Use a trimmed licorice bean for the nose. Makes 6.

be my valentine

Tint 2 tablespoons of buttercream pale pink with 1 drop of red food coloring. Frost the cakes and stick a heart-shaped chocolate in the center. Makes 6.

tiger stripes

Tint 2 tablespoons of buttercream orange with 2 drops of yellow and 1 drop of red food coloring. Trim pieces of licorice wheel to make the eyes, nose, mouth, and ears. Cut thin strips from the orange and black part of licorice allsorts (striped licorice candies) and position around the edges of the cake to make the stripes. Makes 6.

sunny sunflower

Roll out apricot fruit leather to $1/4$ inch thick. Cut out petals with a small, sharp knife. Tint 2 tablespoons of buttercream with 2 drops of yellow food coloring. Frost the cake and arrange the petals on the cake, leaving a small circle in the middle. Fill the circle with chocolate sprinkles. Makes 6.

snake in the grass

Tint 2 tablespoons of buttercream bright green. Put 2 tablespoons shredded coconut in a small bowl and add 2 drops of green food coloring. Stir well until the coconut turns green. Spread green frosting over the cakes and sprinkle with the coconut. Put a gummi snake candy on the cake. Makes 6.

marshmallow flower

Tint 2 tablespoons of buttercream blue with 4–5 drops of blue food coloring. Snip a pink or white marshmallow in half and arrange in a petal pattern. Put a sugar-coated chocolate candy in the center. Makes 6.

out and
about

fighter plane

CAKE AND EQUIPMENT
two 8 x 12 inch rectangular cake pans
3 packages cake mix (35¼ ounces)
copy of template from pages 142–143
toothpicks
18 x 24 inch cake board

DECORATION
2 quantities buttercream from page 11
food colorings: black and red (we used
   powder)
licorice allsorts (striped licorice
   candies)
1 short licorice wheel or licorice strap
6 blue or black licorice beans or
   candies

NOTE
Make sure you check the package size
of the cake mix before you start and
adjust the size accordingly.

1   Preheat the oven to 350°F. Grease the cake pans and line the bases with parchment paper. Divide the cake mix evenly between the pans and bake for 25–30 minutes, or until a skewer inserted into the center of the cakes comes out clean. Let the cakes cool in the pans for 5 minutes before turning out onto a wire rack to cool completely.

2   Tint ¼ cup of the buttercream black and tint the remaining buttercream bright red. Cut out the template pieces, position on the cakes as shown and secure with toothpicks. Cut the cakes to shape and remove the templates and toothpicks.

3   Assemble the bottom layer of the cake on the cake board as shown. Join the nose and tail sections together with a little buttercream, attach the wings to either side of the back part of the nose section, then attach the back wings at the end of the plane's body. Frost this layer red.

4   Shave the cockpit into a dome shape and cover the front section with black buttercream, but leave the rest unfrosted. Assemble the top layer by sitting the cockpit over the nose and joining the cabin to the back of the cockpit. Frost the rest of the top layer red, then sit the tail on top of the end of the plane and frost it red.

5   Cut out 10 black licorice pieces from the licorice allsorts and stick them on the cake as the plane's windows. Cut crosses out of the licorice wheel and position on the wings. Press the licorice beans or candies into the front of the wings—these will be the guns.

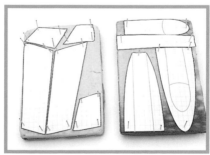

Secure the template pieces onto the cakes with toothpicks.

Join the front wings and the back wings to the side of the bottom layer.

Using a small, sharp knife, shave the cockpit area into a dome.

tippy the dump truck

1 Preheat the oven to 350°F. Grease the loaf pans and line the bases with parchment paper. Divide the cake mix evenly between the pans and bake for 40–45 minutes, or until a skewer inserted into the center of the cakes comes out clean. Let the cakes cool in the pans for 5 minutes before turning out onto a wire rack to cool completely.

2 Cut the lid off an egg carton and trim the edges if necessary so that it will sit flat. Wrap the lid in foil and sit it on the cake board, cut-edge-down—this will support the cake and elevate it. Level one of the cakes, then cut it in half horizontally. With one of the halves of the cake, leave a 5/8 inch border all round and scoop out a shallow hollow—this will be the "tray" of the tip truck.

3 Cut one-third off the other cake. Stand the short piece on its cut side on the front of the egg carton. Stand the longer piece behind the first piece so that together they look like the hood and cabin of the truck. Sit the intact cake half behind the cabin on the back of the egg carton. Join the pieces together with a little buttercream.

4 Put one-third of the buttercream in a bowl and leave it white for the white areas. Tint the remaining buttercream bright red. Spread the red buttercream over the truck, leaving the windshield, windows, and tray unfrosted. Cut the chocolate bars in half diagonally through the long side and place evenly in a line on the base of the truck. This will support the tray of the truck. Put the tray on top of the chocolate bars and frost with the white buttercream. Next, fill in the spaces left for the windows and windshield with white buttercream.

5 Outline the windows and hood with thin strips of licorice and put handles on the doors. Use chocolate-coated cookies for the wheels. Trim the wafer cookie to fit and place it on front of the truck as the grille. Decorate as shown, then fill the tray of the truck with assorted candies.

CAKE AND EQUIPMENT
two 8½ x 4½ x 2¾ inch loaf pans
2 packages cake mix (23½ ounces)
1 cardboard egg carton
6 x 12 inch cake board

DECORATION
1½ quantities buttercream from page 11
red food coloring (we used powder)
2 chocolate-coated caramel snack bars
1 long licorice wheel or licorice strap
6 round chocolate-coated cookies
1 wafer cookie
1½ cups assorted candies

NOTE
Make sure you check the package size of the cake mix before you start and adjust the size accordingly.

Using scissors, cut an egg carton in half; discard the base.

Assemble the tip truck on the foil-covered egg carton.

Sit the tray of the tip truck on top of the layer of chocolate bars.

gnarly dude! skateboard

CAKE AND EQUIPMENT

8 x 12 x 2 inch rectangular roasting pan

2 packages cake mix (23½ ounces)

four 3¼-inch chocolate rolls

8 x 14 inch cake board

copy of template from page 144

toothpicks

ruler

DECORATION

¼ cup dark chocolate chips

¼ cup white chocolate chips

1½ quantities buttercream from page 11

food colorings: green and violet

long green fruit roll-ups

4 dark-colored sugar-coated chocolate candies

NOTE

Make sure you check the package size of the cake mix before you start and adjust the size accordingly.

1 Preheat the oven to 350°F. Grease the roasting pan and line the base with parchment paper. Pour the cake mix into the pan and bake for 35–40 minutes, or until a skewer inserted into the center of the cake comes out clean. Cool in the pan for 5 minutes before turning out onto a wire rack to cool completely.

2 Melt the dark and white chocolate chips separately as described on page 9. Draw some sticker designs onto a sheet of non-stick parchment paper. Lightly oil a baking tray, and turn the paper onto it so that the pencil marks are underneath and the images are backwards.

3 Put the melted dark chocolate into a small paper piping bag, and pipe over the pencil lines. Leave until set. Fill in the outlines with melted white chocolate—the chocolate should be fairly thick but even. Refrigerate until set.

4 Using a serrated knife, level the cake if necessary, then turn over. Position the template on the cake and secure with toothpicks. Cut the cake to shape. Remove the template and toothpicks. Cut down into the blunt end of the skateboard at a 45-degree angle—the small wedge will become the tail.

Once the dark chocolate has set, fill in the outlines with melted white chocolate.

Cut a wedge off the blunt end of the skateboard and keep the wedge.

Put an extra piece of cake in between the wheels to act as extra support.

5 Tint ³/₄ cup of the buttercream pale green. Frost each of the rolls with green buttercream, but leave one end of each unfrosted. Put two rolls on the cake board with the unfrosted ends ¹/₂ inch apart, and sit the other pair parallel, 4¹/₄ inches away. Put a piece of leftover cake, the same height as the rolls, in the gap between the rolls as support for the cake.

6 Tint the remaining buttercream dark violet and cover the skateboard with it. Carefully lift the skateboard onto the wheels. Sit the wedge on the end of the skateboard and cover with violet buttercream.

7 Cut the fruit roll-ups into strips and join them together at the ends to make two strips that are long enough to run down the length of the skateboard. Trim one end of each roll-up on a slight angle to fit the front of the skateboard. Run the two strips parallel down the center of the board. Lift the chocolate "stickers" from the tray and place on the skateboard, right-side-up. Put a sugar-coated chocolate candy in the center of each wheel.

electric guitar

1 Preheat the oven to 350°F. Grease the cake pans and line the bases with parchment paper. Divide the cake mix evenly between the pans and bake for 40–45 minutes, or until a skewer inserted into the center of the cakes comes out clean. Let the cakes cool in the pans for 5 minutes before turning out onto a wire rack to cool completely.

2 Cut one of the cakes into thirds lengthwise and leave the other whole. Position as shown on the cake board, joining the edges with buttercream. Put the template on the cake and secure with toothpicks. Mark the center area, which will be frosted with white buttercream, onto the cake by piercing through the paper with a skewer. Cut the guitar to shape. Remove the template. Trim the guitar's neck if it is too wide. Using one of the offcuts, add some extra length to the guitar's neck, joining with buttercream. Trim the end into a curve. Put 1/2 cup of the white buttercream in a bowl and leave white. Put another 1/2 cup in a bowl and mix with the cocoa powder. Tint the remaining buttercream buttery orange with yellow and red colorings.

3 Frost the middle part of the guitar with white buttercream, using your skewer marks as a guide. Next, frost a 4-inch tip at the end of the neck and the rest of the guitar's body with yellow buttercream. Frost the rest of the neck with brown buttercream. Cut the licorice into strips and outline the white part of the guitar with a thin strip of licorice.

4 Use six pieces of chocolate and six sugar-coated chocolate candies of the same color for the tuning machines and tuning pegs. Cut out two 1/2 x 2 3/4 inch strips of licorice. Lie them across the middle of the cake and add a chocolate licorice bean on either end of them. Cut the licorice wheel into six thin strips about 22 inches long and run them along the length of the guitar for the strings, starting at the first licorice strip and ending where the yellow buttercream on the neck begins. Put a strip of licorice over the end of the strings at the neck end. Decorate the guitar with the remaining candies and halved marshmallow as shown.

CAKE AND EQUIPMENT
two 8 x 12 inch rectangular cake pans
3 packages cake mix (35 1/4 ounces)
12 x 32 inch cake board
copy of template from page 145
toothpicks or skewers
ruler

DECORATION
2 1/2 quantities buttercream from page 11
food colorings: yellow and red
1 tablespoon unsweetened cocoa powder, sifted
two long licorice wheels or licorice straps
1 chocolate bar with triangular pieces
sugar-coated chocolate candies
4 chocolate licorice beans or other bullet-shaped candy
1 marshmallow

NOTE
Make sure you check the package size of the cake mix before you start and adjust the size accordingly.

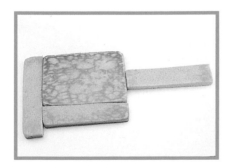

Join the cake strips to the main cake in the basic shape of a guitar.

After you have added an extra piece to the end of the neck, cut it into a curve.

Stick six pieces of chocolate on the end of the guitar.

vroom vroom racing car

CAKE AND EQUIPMENT
8 x 12 inch rectangular cake pan
8¹/₂ x 4¹/₂ x 2³/₄ inch loaf pan
2 packages cake mix (23¹/₂ ounces)
copy of template from page 146
toothpicks
10 x 12 inch cake board

DECORATION
1¹/₂ quantities buttercream from page 11
food colorings: red, yellow, and blue
two long licorice wheels or licorice
    straps
1 yellow candy stick
8 round chocolate cookies
4 mints
2 licorice twists
2 mini gumdrops
1 marshmallow
licorice allsorts (striped licorice candies)
2 yellow aniseed domes

NOTE
Make sure you check the package size
of the cake mix before you
start and adjust the
size accordingly.

1   Preheat the oven to 350°F. Grease the cake pans and line the bases with parchment paper. Divide the cake mix evenly between the pans and bake for 40–45 minutes, or until a skewer inserted into the center of the cakes comes out clean. Let the cakes cool in the pans for 5 minutes before turning out onto a wire rack to cool completely.

2   Put the template of the chassis onto the rectangular cake and secure with toothpicks. Cut to shape, then remove the template and toothpicks. Shape the cake by shaving a slice off either side of it so that the sides taper in. Next, starting from almost halfway along the cake, shave the front at about a 45-degree angle.

3 Put ¼ cup of the buttercream in a small bowl and tint it bright orange by combining red and yellow food colorings. Tint the rest of the buttercream bright blue. Position the chassis in the middle of the cake board and cover it with blue buttercream. Lift the body of the car onto the chassis, then frost it with blue buttercream.

4 Pipe narrow stripes of orange buttercream down the center and sides of the car, then run thin strips of licorice between the stripes. Shape a car number from the candy stick (you could use licorice instead) and attach it to the front of the car.

5 To make a wheel, sandwich two of the chocolate cookies together with a little buttercream and wrap a 7-inch length of licorice wheel around the outside, securing with a trimmed toothpick (make sure you remove the toothpicks before serving). Repeat with the other cookies so that there are four wheels. Attach a mint to the center of each wheel with a little buttercream and position the wheels on the car.

6 To make the rear spoiler, push a toothpick through a 1½-inch licorice twist, through one end of a 4-inch licorice wheel and into a gumdrop. Repeat on the other end of the wheel and stick the spoiler onto the car (again, remove the toothpicks before serving).

7 Use a marshmallow as the helmet. Add details with thin strips of licorice and licorice allsorts. Use the aniseed domes for headlights.

Cut a diagonal slice off the front sides of the cake, then a larger slice off the front.

Lay thin strips of licorice between the piped stripes of orange.

Wrap a licorice strip around each pair of chocolate cookies.

Make the rear spoiler by threading a toothpick through a licorice twist.

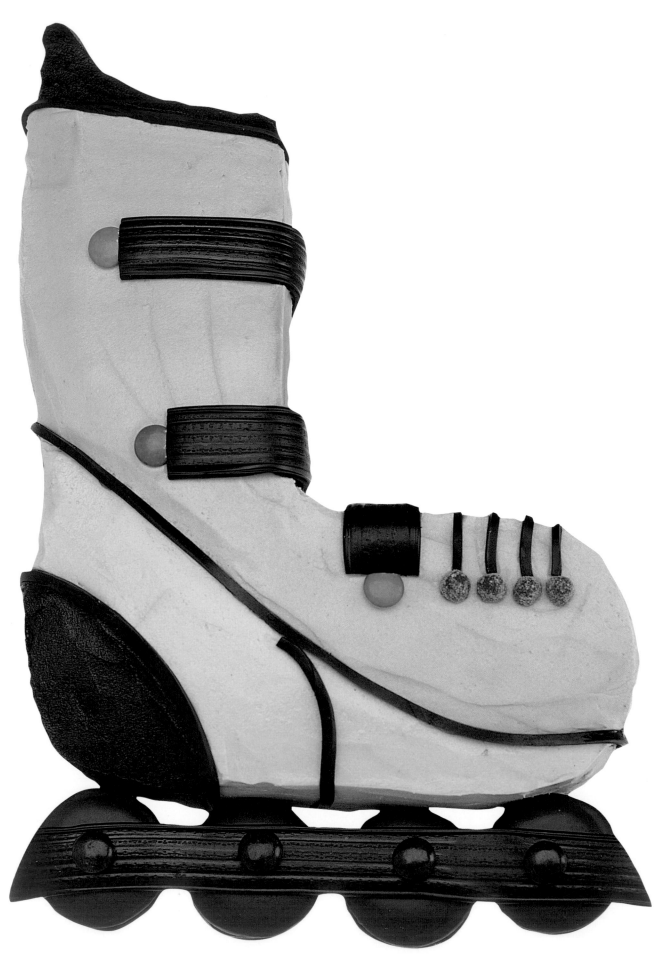

speed demon rollerblade

1. Preheat the oven to 350°F. Grease the cake pan and line the base with parchment paper. Pour the cake mix into the pan and bake for 40–45 minutes, or until a skewer inserted into the center of the cake comes out clean. Cool in the pan for 5 minutes before turning out onto a wire rack to cool completely.

2. Level the cake if necessary. Cut the cake in half, then cut one-third off one of the halves. To assemble the cake, add the shortest piece to the top of the longest, then use the remaining piece for the toe. Join the pieces together with buttercream.

3. Trim the edges of the toe and heel so that the edges are rounded. Next, cut a shallow crescent from the back of the ankle. Finally, cut a small triangular strip off the top of the boot. Turn this triangular strip over to stand on its side and trim if necessary to make it the same height as the rest of the cake. Join the triangle to the top of the boot with a little buttercream.

4. Tint ½ cup of the buttercream black, ½ cup orange, and tint the remaining buttercream bright green. Frost the heel and very top of the boot black. Next, frost a decorative orange stripe in the middle, then frost the rest of the boot bright green.

5. To make the wheels, sandwich pairs of cookies together with a little buttercream and line them along the base of the cake. Put a long strip of licorice over the top of the wheels, securing with a little buttercream. Cut the ends of the licorice into a sharp angle, and stick a black sugar-coated chocolate candy on top of each pair of wheels with a dab of buttercream.

6. To finish, put three strips of licorice of varying lengths on the boot to represent buckles. Cut one curved edge off three blue sugar-coated chocolate candies and stick the flat edge of one against each boot buckle. Cut four very thin strips of licorice for the laces and position as shown, finishing with a mini gumdrop on each end. Cover each of the joins between buttercream colors with a thin strip of licorice, and add one strip to the middle of the orange part.

CAKE AND EQUIPMENT

7½-inch square cake pan
1 package cake mix (11¾ ounces)
12 x 16 inch cake board

DECORATION

2 quantities buttercream from page 11
food colorings: black, orange, and green (we used powder for black)
8 round chocolate-coated cookies
1 long licorice wheel or licorice strap
black and blue sugar-coated chocolate candies
4 red mini gumdrops

NOTE

Make sure you check the package size of the cake mix before you start and adjust the size accordingly.

Cut the cake in half, then cut one third off the end of one of the pieces.

Sit the triangular offcut on its side at the top of the boot.

Stick cookies together with buttercream so that you have four wheels.

choo-choo train

CAKE AND EQUIPMENT

two $8^{1}/_{2}$ x $4^{1}/_{2}$ x $2^{3}/_{4}$ inch loaf pans
$1^{1}/_{2}$ packages cake mix ($17^{1}/_{2}$ ounces)
56 popsicle sticks or coffee stirrers
6 x 22 inch cake board
two 2-inch mini jelly rolls
ruler

DECORATION

2 quantities buttercream from page 11
food colorings: blue, red, and green
1 long licorice wheel or licorice strap
1 large white marshmallow
18 chocolate nonpareils
$1^{1}/_{2}$ cups assorted candies

NOTE
Make sure you check the package size of the cake mix before you start and adjust the size accordingly.

1 Preheat the oven to 350°F. Grease the loaf pans and line the bases with parchment paper. Divide the cake mix evenly between the pans and bake for 35–40 minutes, or until a skewer inserted into the center of the cakes comes out clean. Let the cakes cool in the pans for 5 minutes before turning out onto a wire rack to cool completely.

2 Level the cakes if necessary. Cut one-third off one cake and cut the other cake into three even pieces.

3 To make the track, line up five popsicle sticks end to end along the cake board. Line up another five sticks parallel to the first track. Lay single popsicle sticks across the tracks.

4 To make the engine, sit one of the small pieces of cake on top of the large piece and position on the train track. Use the mini jelly rolls to make the train funnel as shown. To make the carriages, turn the cake pieces upside down and, using a small, sharp knife, hollow out each piece to a depth of $^{5}/_{8}$ inch, leaving a $^{1}/_{2}$-inch border. Line up the carriages on the track behind the engine.

5 Divide the buttercream in half and tint one portion blue. Divide the remaining buttercream into thirds and tint one portion red, one portion purple (by mixing blue and red together), and one portion green. Frost the engine with the blue buttercream, but use one of the other colors for the funnel. Frost each of the wagons a different color.

6 Cut the licorice wheel into thin strips and outline the engine and wagons. Put a marshmallow on the engine's funnel to resemble smoke.

7 Position two chocolate nonpareils along the bottom of each side of the wagons and three along each side of the engine carriage for the wheels. Decorate the train with some of the assorted candies, then generously fill the wagons with them.

Cut one-third off one cake and cut the other one into three equal pieces.

Hollow out each carriage piece, leaving a border, before frosting.

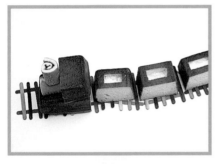
Assemble the cake pieces as shown, lining the carriages behind the engine.

cricket bat and ball

1 Preheat the oven to 350°F. Grease the cake pans and line the bases with parchment paper. Divide the mixture evenly between the pans and bake for 20–25 minutes, or until a skewer inserted into the center of the cakes comes out clean. Let the cakes cool in the pans for 5 minutes before turning out onto a wire rack to cool completely.

2 Cut out the blade and handle templates, position on one of the cakes and secure with a couple of toothpicks. Using a small, sharp knife, cut the cake to shape. Lift the shaped blade (with the template still stuck to it) onto the second cake and align the long edges. Cut the second cake to shape. Use the cookie cutter to cut out a round from the second cake—this will become the cricket ball. Remove the templates and toothpicks and spread some buttercream between the two cakes making up the blade.

3 Using a serrated knife, shape the blade cake into the shape of a house roof by shaving off both long sides diagonally on a 45-degree angle from the center to the edges of the cake. Next, slice a 2-inch slope from each short end of the cake.

4 Join the handle to the top of the blade cake to make a cricket bat. Shave the round of cake into a ball with a small, sharp knife.

5 Tint 1¼ cups of the buttercream caramel brown, ¼ cup red, leave 1 tablespoon white, and tint the remainder black. Frost the blade of the bat with the brown buttercream. Reserve 2 tablespoons of the black buttercream and use the rest to frost the handle. Frost the ball with the red buttercream. Put the white buttercream in a small piping bag and pipe some stitching onto the ball. Put the reserved black buttercream in a small piping bag and outline the cricket bat. Cut out three 2¾-inch strips of red licorice and add decorative strips to the bat.

CAKE AND EQUIPMENT
two 8 x 12 inch rectangular cake pans
2 packages cake mix (23½ ounces)
copy of template from page 147
toothpicks
2¾-inch round cookie cutter
10 x 18 inch cake board
ruler

DECORATION
1 quantity buttercream from page 11
food colorings: caramel, red, and black (we used powder for red)
red licorice laces

NOTE
Make sure you check the package size of the cake mix before you start and adjust the size accordingly.

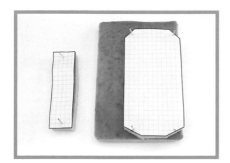
Align the base of the blade along one edge of the second cake.

Shave down the sides of the top cake at a 45-degree angle.

Join the handle to one end of the bat with some buttercream.

the fun boat

CAKE AND EQUIPMENT

two 8¹/2 x 4¹/2 x 2³/4 inch loaf pans
1¹/2 packages cake mix (17¹/2 ounces)
ruler
8 x 14 inch cake board
toothpicks

DECORATION

1¹/2 quantities buttercream from page 11
food colorings: red, blue, and yellow
colored popcorn
fruit rings
sugar-coated chocolate candies
mini gumdrops
two long licorice wheels or licorice
  straps

NOTE

Make sure you check the package size
of the cake mix before you start and
adjust the size accordingly.

1   Preheat the oven to 350°F. Grease the loaf pans and line the bases with parchment paper. Divide the cake mix evenly between the pans and bake for 40–45 minutes, or until a skewer inserted into the center of the cakes comes out clean. Let the cakes cool in the pans for 5 minutes before turning out onto a wire rack to cool completely.

2   Put two-thirds of the buttercream in a small bowl and tint it bright red. Divide the remaining buttercream in two, with one portion larger than the other. Add blue to the larger portion and yellow to the other.

3   Stand the cakes right-side-up. Slice a 2-inch piece from the short ends of one cake (Cake 1), then slice these end pieces horizontally with one piece slightly larger than the other—the larger pieces will become the second deck and the smaller pieces will become the top deck. Cut the other cake (Cake 2) in half and slice the outside corners off at an inward slant.

4   Trim the pieces of cake that will become the top deck so that they are shorter and thinner than the pieces for the deck below. Use the triangular offcuts to cut three cubes for the funnels for the top of the boat.

5   Put the large piece from Cake 1 between the two triangular pieces from Cake 2. Line up the bottom of the two ends from Cake 1 end to end. Do the same with the smaller pieces for the top deck. Move the middle deck onto the top of the bottom deck and the top deck on top of that. Finish with the funnels.

6   Once the cake is assembled, take it apart piece by piece to frost the bottom deck red, the middle deck blue and the top deck yellow. Frost the funnels blue and reassemble the cake on the cake board.

7   Thread three pieces of popcorn onto three toothpicks, trimming the end of each toothpick with scissors (remember to remove the popcorn and toothpicks before serving). Press into the tops of the funnels. Decorate the boat with the candies as shown. Make an anchor out of thin licorice and line the top and bottom of each deck with licorice strips.

Cut the ends off Cake 1 and slice them in half; cut Cake 2 in half and trim the corners.

Line each of the decks up on the cake board in front of you.

Assemble the ship, with each deck centered over the one below.

cartoon fun

bart simpson

CAKE AND EQUIPMENT

two 8 x 12 inch rectangular cake pans
3 packages cake mix (35¼ ounces)
14 x 16 inch cake board
copy of template from page 148
toothpicks or skewers

DECORATION

1½ quantities buttercream from page 11
food colorings: red, black, and yellow
   (we used powder for red and black)
two long licorice wheels or licorice
   straps
1 black jellybean

NOTE

Make sure you check the package size
of the cake mix before you start and
adjust the size accordingly.

1   Preheat the oven to 350°F. Grease the cake pans and line the bases with parchment paper. Divide the cake mix evenly between the pans and bake for 25–30 minutes, or until a skewer inserted into the center of the cakes comes out clean. Let the cakes cool in the pans for 5 minutes before turning out onto a wire rack to cool completely.

2   Sit the cakes on the cake board and join the long edge of one to the long edge of the other with some buttercream. Attach the template to the cake with toothpicks, then cut to shape. Mark the eyes and mouth onto the cake by piercing through the paper with a skewer or toothpicks. Remove the template and toothpicks.

3   Reserve ⅓ cup of the buttercream for the eyes. Tint 1 tablespoon of the remaining buttercream dark red for the tongue, and another tablespoon black for the inside of the mouth—you will only need a small amount of coloring for each. Tint the remaining buttercream bright yellow.

4   Spread the yellow buttercream evenly over the cake, using your skewer marks to show you where to leave the eyes and mouth unfrosted. Use a palette knife to make vertical furrows for the hair. Next, frost the eyes with white buttercream. Transfer the red and black buttercream to separate piping bags and frost the mouth as shown. Once the buttercream is in place, smooth it with a palette knife.

5   Cut the licorice into thin strips, then use these to outline the cake and the features of the face. Cut the jellybean in half and position the halves round-side-up as pupils for the eyes.

Cut the cake to shape and mark the feature lines with a skewer.

Frost the face yellow, leaving the eyes and mouth unfrosted.

Pipe the black and red buttercream for the mouth, then smooth with a palette knife.

MATT GROENING

MATT GROENING

marge simpson

1   Preheat the oven to 350°F. Grease the cake pans and line the bases with parchment paper. Divide the cake mix evenly between the pans and bake for 25–30 minutes, or until a skewer inserted into the center of the cakes comes out clean. Let the cakes cool in the pans for 5 minutes before turning out onto a wire rack to cool completely.

2   Sit the cakes on the cake board and join the short edge of one cake to the short edge of the other with some buttercream. Position the template on the cake as shown and secure with toothpicks. Use a skewer or toothpick to transfer the hairline and eyes onto the cake by piercing through the paper—these lines will help you when you are frosting the cake. Cut the cake to shape. Remove the template and toothpicks.

3   Tint ¼ cup of the buttercream black, leave ¼ cup white, and tint 1 cup bright yellow. Tint the remaining buttercream bright blue.

4   Using your skewer marks as a guide, spread the yellow buttercream over the face, the white buttercream in the eye area, and the blue buttercream over the hair. Use a palette knife to create soft swirls in Marge's hair.

5   Copying the template or picture, use a skewer to mark the outlines of the eyes, nose, mouth, and ear onto the buttercream—if you make a mistake, you can smooth over these marks and redo them. Use your markings as a guide for piping on the features with black buttercream, then pipe around the hair. To dress Marge, make a necklace out of gum balls.

CAKE AND EQUIPMENT

two 8 x 12 inch rectangular cake pans
3 packages cake mix (35¼ ounces)
10 x 22 inch cake board
copy of template from page 149
toothpicks or skewers

DECORATION

2½ quantities buttercream from page 11
food colorings: black, yellow, and blue
   (we used powder for black)
red gum balls

NOTE

Make sure you check the package size of the cake mix before you start and adjust the size accordingly.

Join the cakes along the short sides, then position the template on the cake.

Use a skewer to draw Marge's features onto the frosting.

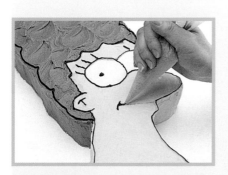

Pipe black buttercream over the guide markings you made for Marge's features.

homer simpson

CAKE AND EQUIPMENT

two 8 x 12 inch rectangular cake pans
3 packages cake mix (35¼ ounces)
14 x 18 inch cake board
copy of template from page 150
toothpicks or skewers

DECORATION

3 quantities buttercream from page 11
food colorings: yellow, brown, red,
   and black (we used powder for
   red and black)
1 large doughnut

NOTE

Make sure you check the package size
of the cake mix before you start and
adjust the size accordingly.

1 Preheat the oven to 350°F. Grease the cake pans and line the bases with parchment paper. Divide the cake mix evenly between the pans and bake for 25–30 minutes, or until a skewer inserted into the center of the cakes comes out clean. Let the cakes cool in the pans for 5 minutes before turning out onto a wire rack to cool completely.

2 Sit the cakes on the cake board. Join the long side of one cake to the short side of the other with a little buttercream, as shown. If necessary, level the bottom cake— the thought cloud doesn't need to be level so you can leave it as it is. Position the template on the cake and secure with toothpicks. Mark any lines separating different buttercream colors onto the cake by piercing through the paper with a skewer or toothpick—these lines will show you where to spread the buttercream. Cut the cake to shape, then remove the template and toothpicks.

3 Tint 1 cup of the buttercream bright yellow, ½ cup dark mustard yellow (by blending a couple of drops of yellow with quite a lot of brown), 1 tablespoon deep red, and ½ cup black. Leave the remaining buttercream white.

4 Spread the buttercream evenly over the cake using the skewer marks as a guide. Start by frosting the eyes, shirt, and thought cloud white. Then spread yellow buttercream over the head, and mustard yellow over the jaw. To finish the frosting, put the red and black buttercream into separate piping bags and pipe red buttercream into the bottom of the mouth and black buttercream into the top of the mouth area. Smooth the buttercream with a palette knife.

5 With the template or picture as a reference, use a skewer to mark the outlines and features onto the frosting. Pipe over these marks with black buttercream. Next, pipe the outline of some thought bubbles (if you are using a colored cake board, fill in the thought bubbles with some white buttercream). Carefully pipe some drool from his mouth. Finally, add Homer's fantasy doughnut to the middle of the thought cloud.

Position the cakes on the cake board, joining them with buttercream.

Use a skewer to mark Homer's features onto the frosting.

Pipe over your skewer outlines with black buttercream.

MATT GROENING

lisa simpson

1 Preheat the oven to 350°F. Grease the cake pans and line the bases with parchment paper. Divide the cake mix evenly between the pans and bake for 25–30 minutes, or until a skewer inserted into the center of the cakes comes out clean. Let the cakes cool in the pans for 5 minutes before turning out onto a wire rack to cool completely.

2 Sit the cakes on the cake board and join the long edge of one cake to the long edge of the other with some buttercream. Position the template on the cake and secure with toothpicks. Use a skewer or toothpick to mark any lines between different colors onto the cake by piercing through the paper. Cut the cake to shape. Remove the template and toothpicks.

3 Leave ¼ cup of the buttercream white. Tint ½ cup of the buttercream bright red. Tint the remaining buttercream bright yellow.

4 Spread the yellow buttercream over the cake using the skewer marks to show you where to leave the cake unfrosted. Next, frost the dress red, then fill in the eyes with white buttercream. Cut long, thin strips of licorice and use them to outline the eyelashes, eyes, ear, dress, nose, and mouth. Use more of the licorice to outline the edges of the cake.

5 To dress Lisa, make a necklace out of gum balls and position as shown. Cut the jellybean in half and place round-side-up as the pupils.

CAKE AND EQUIPMENT
two 8 x 12 inch rectangular cake pans
3 packages cake mix (35¼ ounces)
12 x 16 inch cake board
copy of template from page 151
toothpicks or skewers

DECORATION
2 quantities buttercream from page 11
food colorings: red and yellow (we used powder for red)
two long licorice wheels or licorice straps
5 large white gum balls or white chocolate balls
1 black jellybean

NOTE
Make sure you check the package size of the cake mix before you start and adjust the size accordingly.

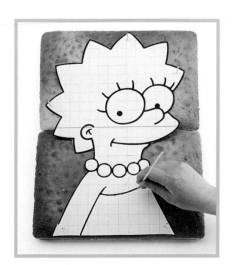

Mark the outline of the eyes and dress onto the cake.

Once you have frosted the face, fill in the eyes with white buttercream.

Cut a jellybean in half and press, round-side-up, into Lisa's eyes.

maggie simpson

CAKE AND EQUIPMENT

two 8 x 12 inch rectangular cake pans
3 packages cake mix (35¼ ounces)
12 x 16 inch cake board
copy of template from page 152
toothpicks or skewers

DECORATION

2 quantities buttercream from page 11
food colorings: red, blue, and yellow
   (we used powder for red)
two long licorice wheels or licorice
   straps
1 black jellybean

NOTE
Make sure you check the package size
of the cake mix before you start and
adjust the size accordingly.

1　Preheat the oven to 350°F. Grease the cake pans and line the bases with parchment paper. Divide the cake mix evenly between the pans and bake for 25–30 minutes, or until a skewer inserted into the center of the cakes comes out clean. Let the cakes cool in the pans for 5 minutes before turning out onto a wire rack to cool completely.

2　Sit the cakes on the cake board and join the long edge of one cake to the long edge of the other with some buttercream. Position the template on the cake as shown, secure with toothpicks and cut the cake to shape. Referring to the picture, mark any lines separating different colored frostings onto the cake by piercing through the paper with a skewer or toothpick—these lines will help you when you are spreading on the frosting. Remove the template and toothpicks.

3　Reserve 2 tablespoons of white buttercream for the eyes. Tint ¼ cup of the buttercream dark red for the dummy. Divide the remaining buttercream in half and tint one portion bright blue and the other bright yellow.

4　Spread the yellow buttercream over the hands and face, leaving the eye area unfrosted. Next, cover the baby outfit with blue buttercream. Fill in the area for the eyes with white buttercream. Using a skewer, mark the outline of the dummy and hair bow onto the frosting. Put the remaining blue buttercream in a piping bag and pipe on the hair bow, then smooth with a palette knife. Put the red buttercream in a piping bag and fill in the area you have marked out for the dummy. Smooth the buttercream with a palette knife.

5　Cut the licorice wheels into thin strips and use to outline the features and the edges of the cake. Cut the jellybean in half and position round-side-up for the pupils.

Use a small knife to cut around the edge of the template.

Fill the space for the eyes with white buttercream.

Outline Maggie and her features with thin strips of licorice.

MATT GROENING

MATT GROENING

santa's little helper

1 Preheat the oven to 350°F. Grease the cake pans and line the bases with parchment paper. Divide the cake mix evenly between the pans and bake for 25–30 minutes, or until a skewer inserted into the center of the cakes comes out clean. Let the cakes cool in the pans for 5 minutes before turning out onto a wire rack to cool completely.

2 Sit the cakes on the cake board and join the long edge of one cake to the long edge of the other with some buttercream. Position the template on the cake, secure with toothpicks and cut the cake to shape. Transfer the outline of the eyes and nose onto the cake by piercing through the paper with a skewer or toothpick. Remove the template and toothpicks. Attach the tail to the board by spreading some of the buttercream underneath the cake.

3 Reserve 1–2 tablespoons of white buttercream for the eyes. Tint 3 tablespoons of the buttercream black. Tint the remaining buttercream an orange brown color by blending brown and red food colorings.

4 Spread the buttercream evenly over the cake using the skewer marks as a guide—white for the eyes, black for the nose, and brown for the rest of the cake. You might find it easier to frost the nose and eyes first.

5 Copying from the template or picture, draw the features onto the frosting with a skewer—if you make a mistake, smooth over the lines and redo them. Carefully pipe over these marks with black buttercream.

CAKE AND EQUIPMENT

two 8 x 12 inch rectangular cake pans
3 packages cake mix (35¼ ounces)
14 x 16 inch cake board
copy of template from page 153
toothpicks or skewers

DECORATION

1½ quantities buttercream from page 11
food colorings: black, brown, and red
   (we used powder for black)

NOTE

Make sure you check the package size of the cake mix before you start and adjust the size accordingly.

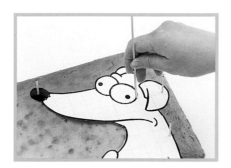

Pierce through the template with a skewer to outline the eyes and nose.

Secure the tail to the cake board with a little buttercream.

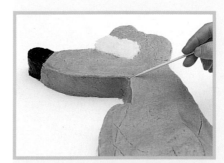

Mark the features onto the frosting with a skewer.

mr. montgomery burns

CAKE AND EQUIPMENT

two 8 x 12 inch rectangular cake pans

3 packages cake mix (35¼ ounces)

12 x 18 inch cake board

copy of template from page 154

toothpicks or skewers

DECORATION

3 quantities buttercream from page 11

food colorings: yellow, red, black, and
  green (we used powder for red, but
  liquid for black to achieve gray)

NOTE

Make sure you check the package size
of the cake mix before you start and
adjust the size accordingly.

1 Preheat the oven to 350°F. Grease the cake pans and line the bases with parchment paper. Divide the cake mix evenly between the pans and bake for 25–30 minutes, or until a skewer inserted into the center of the cakes comes out clean. Let the cakes cool in the pans for 5 minutes before turning out onto a wire rack to cool completely.

2 Put the cakes together on a cake board as shown, joining the edges with a little buttercream. Position the template on the cake and secure with toothpicks. Mark any lines separating different frosting colors onto the cake by piercing through the paper with a skewer or toothpick. Cut the cake to shape, then remove the template and toothpicks.

3 Reserve ⅓ cup white buttercream for the eyes, shirt, and teeth. Tint 1½ cups buttercream bright yellow, 2 tablespoons deep red, ½ cup gray using a little of the black food coloring, and the remaining buttercream bright green for the jacket.

4 Using your skewer marks as a guide, frost Mr. Burns with white buttercream for the eyes, mouth, shirt, and cuffs. Then use yellow buttercream for the hands and head, and smooth with a palette knife. Spread gray buttercream over the hair, but reserve about 3 tablespoons. Use the green buttercream for the jacket. Next, transfer the red buttercream to a piping bag and pipe it onto the tie. Use 1 tablespoon of the reserved gray buttercream to pipe on the spots on the head.

5 Tint the remaining gray buttercream black by adding more black coloring. Copying the template or picture, use a skewer to mark the features of the face and body onto the frosting—if you make a mistake, smooth over and start again. Pipe over these markings and the outline with black buttercream.

Transfer the features from the template onto the cake by piercing with a skewer.

Spread the buttercream onto the cake with a palette knife

Using your skewer marks as a guide, pipe the features with black buttercream.

MATT GROENING

MATT GROENING

head to toe bart simpson

1 Preheat the oven to 350°F. Grease the cake pans and line the bases with parchment paper. Divide the cake mix evenly between the pans and bake for 25–30 minutes, or until a skewer inserted into the center of the cakes comes out clean. Let the cakes cool in the pans for 5 minutes before turning out onto a wire rack to cool completely.

2 Sit the cakes on the cake board and join the long edge of one cake to the long edge of the other with some buttercream. Position the template on the cake and secure with toothpicks. Use a skewer or toothpick to mark out the lines between frosting colors onto the cake by piercing through the paper—you will need to refer to the picture to do this. Cut the cake to shape, then remove the template and toothpicks.

3 Put 1/3 cup of the buttercream in a bowl and leave it white. Place 2/3 cup of the buttercream in one bowl and tint it deep red. Put 1/2 cup in another bowl and tint it deep blue, then tint another 1/2 cup black. Tint the remaining large quantity bright yellow.

4 Spread the buttercream evenly over the cake using the skewer marks as a guide—white for the eyes; yellow for the head, arms, and legs; blue for the shorts and shoes, and red for the T-shirt. Put the remaining white buttercream in a small piping bag and pipe it quite thickly over the shoe soles, side dots, and socks.

5 Copying the template or picture, outline the features with a skewer, then pipe over your skewer marks with black buttercream. Next, pipe around the edges of the cake. To finish Bart, add two dots of black buttercream for the pupils of his eyes.

CAKE AND EQUIPMENT
two 8 x 12 inch rectangular cake pans
3 packages cake mix (35 1/4 ounces)
14 x 18 inch cake board
copy of template from page 155
toothpicks or skewers

DECORATION
3 quantities buttercream from page 11
food colorings: red, blue, black, and yellow (we used powder for red and black)

NOTE
Make sure you check the package size of the cake mix before you start and adjust the size accordingly.

Mark out the lines between frosting colors with a skewer.

Using your skewer marks as a guide, frost Bart with a palette knife.

Add detailing to Bart's shoes by piping with white buttercream.

itchy & scratchy

CAKE AND EQUIPMENT

two 8 x 12 inch rectangular cake pans

3 packages cake mix (35¼ ounces)

16-inch square cake board

copy of template from page 156

toothpicks or skewers

DECORATION

2 quantities buttercream from page 11

food colorings: blue, yellow, red, and
   black (we used powder for red
   but liquid for black to get gray)

two long licorice wheels or licorice
   straps

2 black jellybeans

2 mini white marshmallows, cut in half

NOTE

Make sure you check the package size
of the cake mix before you start and
adjust the size accordingly.

1 Preheat the oven to 350°F. Grease the cake pans and line the bases with parchment paper. Divide the cake mix evenly between the pans and bake for 25–30 minutes, or until a skewer inserted into the center of the cakes comes out clean. Let the cakes cool in the pans for 5 minutes before turning out onto a wire rack to cool completely.

2 Sit the long edge of each cake next to one another on a cake board, with the cake on the right slightly lower than the cake on the left. Join the edges with buttercream. Put the template on the cake, secure with toothpicks and cut the cake to shape. Referring to the picture, transfer any lines between different frosting colors onto the cake by piercing through the paper with a skewer or toothpick. Remove the template and toothpicks.

3 Spread about 1 tablespoon of white buttercream in the area marked out for Itchy's (the mouse's) eyes. Tint ¾ cup of the buttercream blue and spread it all over Itchy's face.

4 Next, move on to Scratchy (the cat). Tint 1½ tablespoons of the buttercream a pale yellow and fill in the eyes. Tint 1 tablespoon of the buttercream red and set it aside. Tint 2 tablespoons of the buttercream pale gray and set it aside. Tint the remaining buttercream dark gray. Spread the dark gray buttercream over Scratchy's face, reserving 1 tablespoon for later use. Next, spread the red buttercream into the area for the tongue. To finish, spread the light gray buttercream into the area for Scratchy's nose. Use the remaining dark gray buttercream to frost Itchy's nose, then smooth all the buttercream with a palette knife.

5 Cut the licorice wheels into thin strips and outline the whole cake and the features as shown. Cut two jellybeans in half and position round-side-up as the pupils of the eyes. Place the halved marshmallows in place for the teeth.

Sit the cakes side by side; the one on the left slightly higher than the right.

Pierce the paper with a skewer to mark lines between frosting colors.

MATT GROENING

Smooth the gray buttercream onto the cake in the area marked out for the nose.

Outline the cake with thin strips of licorice.

MATT GROENING

Sit the template on the two cakes, then cut off the top right corner.

Move the corner offcut to the bottom of the cake under Krusty's bow tie.

Give the impression of curly hair by softly swirling the green frosting.

krusty the clown

1 Preheat the oven to 350°F. Grease the cake pans and line the bases with parchment paper. Divide the cake mix evenly between the pans and bake for 25–30 minutes, or until a skewer inserted into the center of the cakes comes out clean. Let the cakes cool in the pans for 5 minutes before turning out onto a wire rack to cool completely.

2 Put the long sides of the two cakes together on a cake board, joining the edges with a little buttercream. Sit the template on the cake and secure with toothpicks—his neck won't fit on yet. Cut off the top right corner of the cake as shown and move it underneath Krusty's neck, then join with a little buttercream. Use a skewer or toothpick to mark all the lines between different frosting colors onto the cake by piercing through the paper—you will need to refer to the picture to do this. Cut the cake to shape, then remove the template and toothpicks.

3 Put $1/4$ cup of the buttercream in a bowl and leave it white. Put $2/3$ cup of the buttercream in a bowl and, adding one drop at a time, tint it very pale yellow. Tint $1/2$ cup of the buttercream caramel. Set five cups next to one another and divide the buttercream among them as follows: the first two cups each have 1 tablespoon of buttercream, then the next three cups each have 2 tablespoons of buttercream. Tint them deep red, gray, purple, blue, and black, respectively. Tint the remaining buttercream bright green.

4 Pipe or spread the white buttercream in the areas marked out for the eyes and teeth. Next, spread the yellow buttercream over the neck and the top of the face. Spread the caramel buttercream over the jaw. Spread the red buttercream in the area marked out for the nose and tongue, and the gray for inside the mouth. Spread the purple over the collar and carefully make the bow tie blue. Spread the green buttercream over the hair and gently swirl with a palette knife to give the impression of curls.

5 Outline all of Krusty's features with a skewer. Using the skewer marks as a guide, pipe black buttercream over the features and edges of the cake. To finish Krusty, add two dots of black for the pupils of the eyes.

CAKE AND EQUIPMENT
two 8 x 12 inch rectangular cake pans
3 packages cake mix (35$1/4$ ounces)
14 x 18 inch cake board
copy of template from page 157
toothpicks or skewers

DECORATION
2$1/2$ quantities buttercream from page 11
food colorings: yellow, caramel, red,
   gray, purple, blue, black, and green
   (we used powder for red and black)

NOTE
Make sure you check the package size of the cake mix before you start and adjust the size accordingly.

count to ten

first birthday blocks

CAKE AND EQUIPMENT
two 10 x 3 x 5 inch loaf pans
1 package cake mix (11¾ ounces)
6 x 16 inch cake board
skewer or toothpick

DECORATION
2 quantities buttercream from page 11
food colorings: red, blue, yellow, and
  green

NOTE
Make sure you check the package size
of the cake mix before you start and
adjust the size accordingly.

1 Preheat the oven to 350°F. Grease the loaf pans and line the bases with parchment paper. Divide the cake mix evenly between the pans and bake for 35 minutes, or until a skewer inserted into the center of the cakes comes out clean. Let the cakes cool in the pans for 5 minutes before turning out onto a wire rack to cool completely.

2 Level both cakes. Leave one cake whole and cut the other cake in half, then slice a small triangle off one of the halves. Put the pieces on the cake board in the shape of a figure one—you will not need the leftover triangle of the cut cake. Join the edges with a little buttercream.

3 Take out four ¼-cup portions of the buttercream and put each into a small bowl. Tint one portion red, another blue, one portion yellow, and the final portion green. Spoon each color into a small piping bag. Leave the largest portion of the buttercream white.

4 Spread white buttercream over the entire surface of the cake, including the sides; spread smoothly with a palette knife. Use a skewer to outline the cubes and mark letters and numbers in the center of the cubes—we have used random characters but you could use your child's initials.

5 Pipe over your skewer marks on each cube, alternating the colors of the frosting so that each cube is a different color. Then, carefully fill in the center of the letters and numbers with the same color you used for the outline.

Leave one cake whole and cut the other one into three pieces.

Move the cake into position to form the number one.

Draw the outlines, then fill with the same color of buttercream.

snakey number two

1 Preheat the oven to 350°F. Grease the loaf pans and line the bases with parchment paper. Divide the cake mix evenly between the pans and bake for 45 minutes, or until a skewer inserted into the center of the cakes comes out clean. Let the cakes cool in the pans for 5 minutes before turning out onto a wire rack to cool completely.

2 Do not trim the tops of cakes—leave the cakes rounded to form the shape of a snake. Position the template pieces onto the cakes and secure with toothpicks. Cut the cakes to shape, then assemble cake pieces A–E (from the template) into the shape of a snake. Remove the template and toothpicks and join the pieces together with a little buttercream.

3 Put 2 tablespoons of the buttercream in a small bowl and tint it dark violet, similar to the color of the sprinkles. Spoon the violet buttercream into a piping bag. Tint the remaining buttercream bright green.

4 Spread the green buttercream evenly over the entire cake, using a palette knife to smooth the surface. Once the snake has been completely frosted with the green buttercream, pipe squiggly patches over the snake with the violet buttercream. Fill the insides of the patches with purple sprinkles.

5 Put the jellybeans in place for the eyes. Pipe a little violet buttercream onto the jellybean and stick a purple sugar-coated candy to the front of it. Pipe on a mouth with violet buttercream, then pipe two dots for the nostrils. Make a slit in the head part of the red gummi snake for the tip of the tongue and trim so that it is only about 1 1/4 inches long. Insert into the mouth of the cake snake.

CAKE AND EQUIPMENT
10 x 3 x 5 inch loaf pan
8-inch ring pan
2 packages cake mix (23 1/2 ounces)
copy of template from page 158
toothpicks
12-inch square cake board

DECORATION
2 quantities buttercream from page 11
food colorings: violet and green
purple sprinkles
2 white jellybeans
2 purple sugar-coated chocolate candies
1 red gummi snake

NOTE
Make sure you check the package size of the cake mix before you start and adjust the size accordingly.

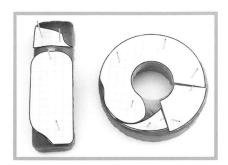
Stick the template pieces onto the cakes with a few toothpicks.

Move the cake pieces into position in the shape of a snake.

Fill in the violet outlines with purple sprinkles.

third bird-day

CAKE AND EQUIPMENT
two 8-inch ring pans
2 packages cake mix (23 1/2 ounces)
13 x 13 inch cake board

DECORATION
1 1/2 quantities buttercream from page 11
food colorings: red and yellow
yellow and white jellybeans
banana candies
1 marshmallow
1 black jellybean
2 orange gummi snakes

NOTE
Make sure you check the package size of the cake mix before you start and adjust the size accordingly.

1 Preheat the oven to 350°F. Grease the cake pans and line the bases with parchment paper. Divide the mixture evenly between the pans and bake for 40–45 minutes, or until a skewer inserted into the center of the cakes comes out clean. Let the cakes cool in the pans for 5 minutes before turning out onto a wire rack to cool completely.

2 Do not level the cakes—leave them rounded. Cut one ring cake in half, with one end pointed for the beak, as shown. Cut a small piece from the middle of the other ring cake. Join the piece with the pointed end to the larger piece in the shape of a figure three.

3 Tint 1/4 cup of the buttercream bright orange-red. Tint the remaining buttercream bright yellow. Spread some orange buttercream over the end of the top cake for the beak. Add a couple more drops of red to the leftover orange buttercream and frost a strip along the bottom of the beak for the opening of the mouth. Frost the rest of the cake with yellow buttercream. Alternatively, you may prefer to frost all of the cake with the yellow buttercream first and then go over the beak area with the orange buttercream.

4 Cut the jellybeans and bananas in half lengthwise. Leave a small space behind the beak for the eyes, then start laying jellybeans over the buttercream, cut-side-down. Stop when you reach the middle point of the three. Stick four rows of bananas in the middle of the cake. Add another five rows or so of jellybeans beneath the bananas, then add another three rows of bananas.

5 Cut a marshmallow in half and use it for the eyes. Cut the ends off a black jellybean and place rounded-side-up on the marshmallows, using a little buttercream to stick them in place. Add plumage by sticking a few bananas at a jaunty angle behind the eyes. Make three slits on the head end of the gummi snakes to create feet, then place them on the bottom of the cake as shown. Overlap some bananas on top of the legs to hide the top ends.

Cut the two ring cakes into the shapes as shown.

Carefully place the jellybeans on the cake, slightly layering them.

Snip the end of a snake into three thin strips so that they look like bird legs.

race you four it!

1. Preheat the oven to 350°F. Grease the loaf pans and line the bases with parchment paper. Divide the cake mix evenly among the pans and bake for 35 minutes, or until a skewer inserted into the center of the cakes comes out clean. Let the cakes cool in the pans for 5 minutes before turning out onto a wire rack to cool completely.

2. Leave one cake whole. Cut the second cake in half, then cut one of the halves in half again. For the last cake, cut a small slice from one end, then cut a triangle off each end of the larger piece. Arrange the cake pieces on the cake board in the shape of a figure four as shown, leveling the cake if necessary, and trimming any pieces that are a little too large. Join the edges with a little buttercream.

3. Reserve ¼ cup of the white buttercream and tint the remaining buttercream caramel brown. Spread the white buttercream over the blaze (the light-colored mark on the face of the horse). Spread brown buttercream over the rest of the horse and blend it neatly into the white frosting.

4. Using a skewer, mark onto the buttercream the mouth, mane, the inside and outside of the ear, and the large comma shape for the nostril. Spread some of the white buttercream into the mouth area, then into the center of the ear. Build up the height of the outer area of the ear with more brown buttercream.

5. Melt the chocolate as described on page 9. Spoon the melted chocolate into a piping bag, then pipe over your skewer marks to form an outline around the mane, ear, and nostril. Fill the mane with chocolate sprinkles. Continue the mane down the side of the cake by carefully pushing sprinkles onto the side of the cake.

6. To make the eye, stick a brown candy to a mint with a little buttercream. Cut an eyelash out of a ⅝-inch piece of licorice and put it above the eye, fanning out the lashes. Cut thin strips from the licorice and line the mouth of the horse. Arrange fruit roll-ups for reins and yellow candies for the studs.

CAKE AND EQUIPMENT
three 10 x 3 x 5 inch loaf pans
1½ packages cake mix (17½ ounces)
13 x 13 inch cake board
ruler

DECORATION
1½ quantities buttercream from page 11
brown food coloring
⅓ cup dark chocolate chips
chocolate sprinkles
1 brown sugar-coated chocolate candy
1 round mint
1 short licorice wheel or licorice strap
long red fruit roll-ups
2 yellow sugar-coated chocolate candies

NOTE
Make sure you check the package size of the cake mix before you start and adjust the size accordingly.

Leave one cake intact and cut the other two as shown.

Move the pieces into the shape of a four and join the pieces with buttercream.

Use a palette knife to push chocolate sprinkles up the side of the cake.

five down on the farm

CAKE AND EQUIPMENT
10 x 3 x 5 inch loaf pan
8-inch ring pan
1½ packages cake mix (17½ ounces)
10 x 20 inch cake board
ruler

DECORATION
1½ quantities buttercream from page 11
food colorings: caramel and green
blue cake decorating gel
2/3 cup dark or milk chocolate chips
plastic farm animals or assorted animal
   candies

NOTES
If you don't have any farm animals
in the toy box, try the toy store. Most
toy stores have a toy section where
you can buy inexpensive toys that will
be perfect for this cake.

Make sure you check the package size
of the cake mix before you start and
adjust the size accordingly.

1 Preheat the oven to 350°F. Grease the cake pans and line the bases with
   parchment paper. Divide the cake mix evenly between the pans and bake for
   45 minutes, or until a skewer inserted into the center of the cakes comes out
   clean. Let the cakes cool in the pans for 5 minutes before turning out onto a
   wire rack to cool completely.

2 Cut the loaf cake in half. Cut a piece from the ring cake that is almost a
   quarter of the ring. Next, square off this piece by neatly cutting off the
   rounded edges. Arrange the pieces on the cake board in the shape of a figure
   five, using the smaller offcuts to lengthen the top loaf of the number. Join the
   edges with a little buttercream.

3 Put ¾ cup of the buttercream in a small bowl and tint it light brown for the
   ground cover; tint the remaining buttercream light green for the grass.

4 Mark out three sections for the paddocks, then spread green buttercream over
   the top and bottom sections, and brown over the middle section. Make a pond
   by piping blue food gel onto one of the green paddocks.

5 Put the chocolate in a heatproof bowl. Bring a saucepan of water to the boil,
   then remove from the heat. Sit the bowl over the pan, making sure the base
   of the bowl does not sit in the water. Stir occasionally until the chocolate has
   melted. Spoon the chocolate into a piping bag and create a mud bath for the
   pigs by piping some of the chocolate into the middle paddock.

6 Pipe the remaining chocolate onto a sheet of parchment paper that has been
   placed on an oiled baking tray. Pipe about 30 fences (this will allow for any
   breakages), each about 1¼ x 2 inches in size. When set, carefully stick the
   fences around the edge of the cake. Decorate the cake with farm animals
   or candies of your choice.

Slice off the rounded edges from the side
and top of the piece from the ring cake.

Position the cake pieces into the shape
of a figure five.

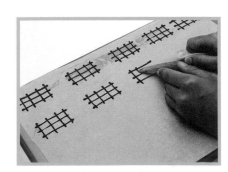

Pipe fences about 1¼ inches high and
2 inches wide out of melted chocolate.

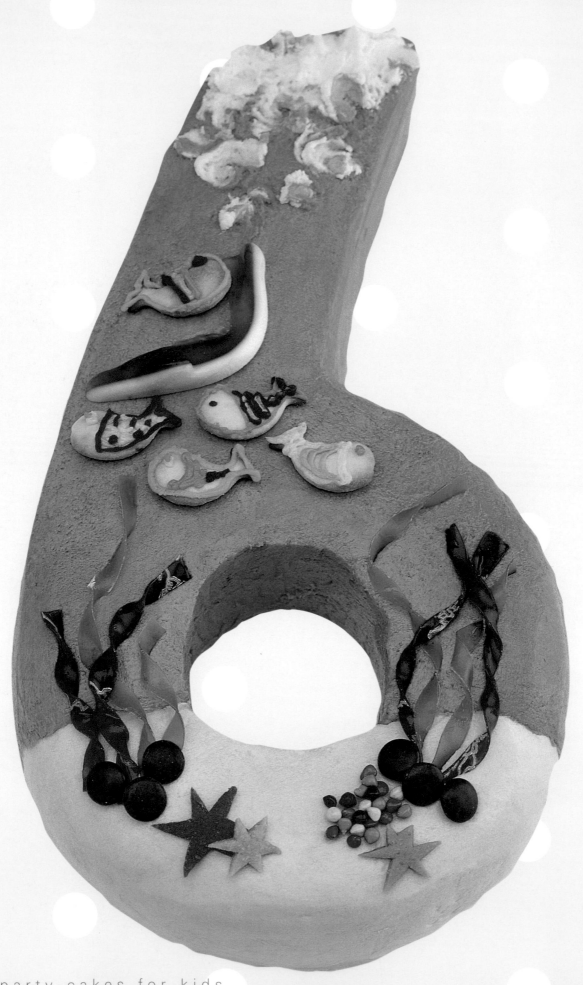

under the sea at six

1   Preheat the oven to 350°F. Grease the cake pans and line the bases with parchment paper. Divide the cake mix evenly between the pans and bake for 45 minutes, or until a skewer inserted into the center of the cakes comes out clean. Let the cakes cool in the pans for 5 minutes before turning out onto a wire rack to cool completely.

2   Leave the ring cake whole and cut the loaf cake as shown. Arrange the cakes on the cake board in the shape of a figure six, discarding the offcuts and joining the edges with buttercream. Trim to neaten the edges and the top of the cake.

3   Reserve 1/4 cup of the white buttercream in a small bowl. Place 1/2 cup of buttercream in another bowl and tint it caramel to resemble sand. Tint the remaining buttercream blue.

4   Spread sand-colored buttercream over the bottom of the figure six, then cover the rest of the cake with the blue buttercream. Spread some of the white buttercream at the top to resemble a wave—use a palette knife to rough up the white buttercream so that it looks more realistic.

5   Cut green and red fruit roll-ups into various lengths, then twist the strips a few times so that they look like seaweed strands. Stick the seaweed onto the cake, inserting them into the sand-colored buttercream. Put brown sugar-coated chocolate candies at the base of each plant to represent rocks.

6   Cut the colored section away from the licorice allsorts and using a small star cutter or small, sharp knife, cut star shapes from them. Put the starfish on the sand. Sprinkle some rainbow choc chips onto the sand to add more color. Let your imagination run wild and decorate the cake with fish-shaped candies, toys, and crackers, using cake decorating gel or colored buttercream to make features and patterns on the fish.

CAKE AND EQUIPMENT
10 x 3 x 5 inch loaf pan
8-inch ring pan
1 1/2 packages cake mix (17 1/2 ounces)
10 x 18 inch cake board

DECORATION
1 1/2 quantities buttercream from page 11
food colorings: caramel and blue
green and red fruit roll-ups
brown sugar-coated chocolate candies
    or other brown candies
licorice allsorts (striped licorice
    candies)
rainbow choc chips or other rainbow
    candies
assorted fish-shaped candies and
    sea-themed toys
goldfish crackers
cake decorating gels: assorted colors

NOTE
Make sure you check the package size of the cake mix before you start and adjust the size accordingly.

Cut a sharp curve in the bottom of the loaf cake and a soft curve at the top.

Join the loaf cake to the ring cake with some buttercream.

Add swirls of white buttercream to resemble waves crashing on rocks.

seventh heaven

CAKE AND EQUIPMENT

two 10 x 3 x 5 inch loaf pans
1 package cake mix (11³/4 ounces)
13-inch square cake board

DECORATION

1¹/2 quantities buttercream from page 11
food colorings: blue and green
2 teaspoons unsweetened cocoa
   powder
³/4 cup candied fruit leaves
2 flaked chocolate bars
banana candies
toy monkeys or monkey candies

NOTE

Make sure you check the package size
of the cake mix before you start and
adjust the size accordingly.

1 Preheat the oven to 350°F. Grease the loaf pans and line the bases with
parchment paper. Divide the cake mix evenly between the pans and bake for
35 minutes, or until a skewer inserted into the center of the cakes comes out
clean. Let the cakes cool in the pans for 5 minutes before turning out onto a
wire rack to cool completely.

2 Trim the cakes as shown so that the top loaf cake has three corners cut off
(but not the corner that will join the bottom cake), and the second cake
has a diagonal strip cut off one end and the corners cut off the other end.
Arrange the pieces on the cake board in the shape of a figure seven, joining
the edges with a little buttercream.

3 Put ¹/4 cup of the buttercream in a small bowl and tint it blue for the sky.
Divide the remaining buttercream in half. Tint one half green, and add the
cocoa to the other half and mix together to create a deep brown.

4 Spread a 2-inch strip of blue buttercream at each end of the top of the figure
seven and fill in the space with green buttercream. Then, cover the trunk with
the brown buttercream.

5 Cut the candied fruit leaves in half horizontally with sharp scissors and overlap
on the green buttercream, with a few edging over the blue buttercream—it
looks nice to have the leaves mainly sugar-side-up, but with occasional ones
shiny-side-up. Break the chocolate bars into flakes and sprinkle over the trunk
of the tree, pressing down lightly into the buttercream so that they stay in
place. Arrange assorted bananas in a bunch just below the leaves—we used
small and large bananas, but you can use just one kind if you prefer. For the
final touch, add your monkeys or other jungle animal to the tree.

Cut the corners off the cakes where shown
and make a diagonal slice off one cake.

Join the cakes together to form the shape
of a seven.

Frost the sky blue, the leaves green, and
the trunk brown.

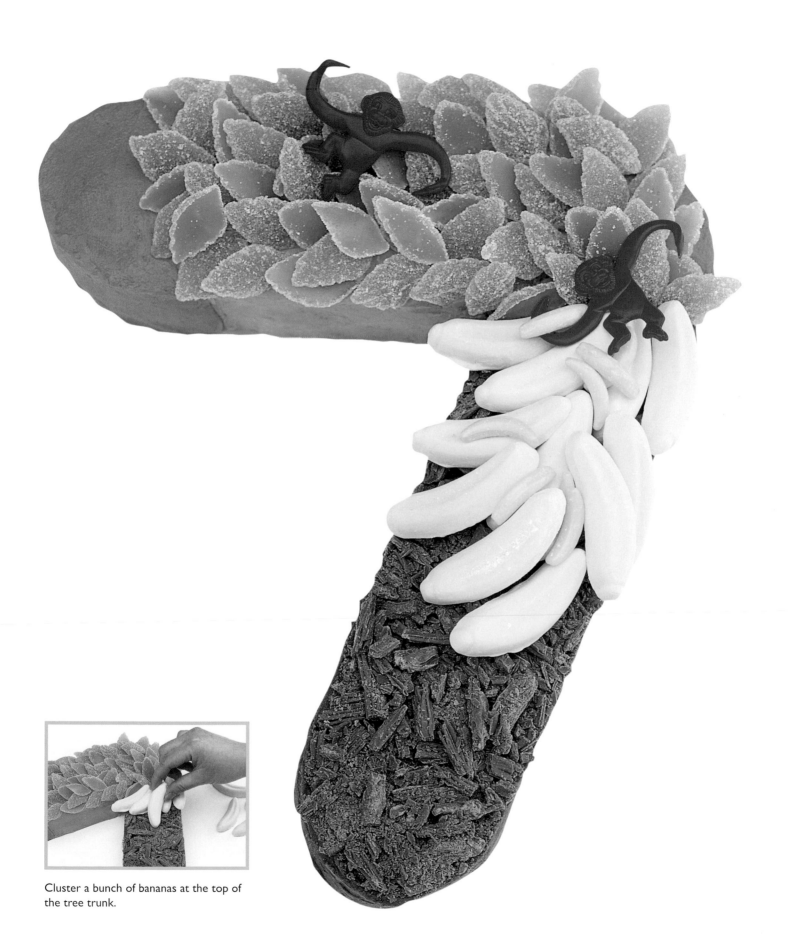

Cluster a bunch of bananas at the top of
the tree trunk.

racing at eight

1 Preheat the oven to 350°F. Grease the cake pans and line the bases with parchment paper. Divide the cake mix evenly between the pans and bake for 40 minutes, or until a skewer inserted into the center of the cakes comes out clean. Let the cakes cool in the pans for 5 minutes before turning out onto a wire rack to cool completely.

2 Cut a small slice off each cake as shown so that they will sit flat against each other. Arrange the cakes on the cake board in the shape of a figure eight, joining the edges with a little buttercream. Trim to neaten the edges and the top of the cake. Tint the buttercream green, then spread evenly over the cake.

3 Use black licorice to mark out the lanes of the racing track and add a strip across the finish line. Cut the red licorice into short strips about ³/₄ inch long (you will need about 35). Put the red strips in a line running down the center of each lane. Put bear cookies and gummy bears at the edges of the track for the cheering crowd. Put cars on the track and insert flags (paper or made from toothpicks and licorice allsort slices) at the finish line and at other points around the track.

CAKE AND EQUIPMENT
two 8-inch ring pans
2 packages cake mix (23¹/₂ ounces)
12 x 20 inch cake board
ruler

DECORATION
2 quantities buttercream from page 11
green food coloring
two long licorice wheels or licorice straps
red licorice laces
tiny bear cookies or other tiny animal cookies
gummy bears
chocolate or toy cars
flags or licorice allsorts (striped licorice candies) and toothpicks

NOTE
Make sure you check the package size of the cake mix before you start and adjust the size accordingly.

Cut a small slice off both of the cakes so that they can sit flat against one another.

Push the cakes together on a cake board and join the edges with buttercream.

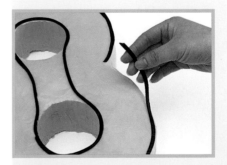
Outline the track with thin strips of black licorice.

lift off! nine

CAKE AND EQUIPMENT

8-inch ring pan

10 x 3 x 5 inch loaf pan

1½ packages cake mix (17½ ounces)

10 x 18 inch cake board

DECORATION

2 quantities buttercream from page 11

food colorings: black and blue (we used
gel for both)

1 pound 2 ounce package ready-made
frosting

1 ice cream cone

dragées

colored sprinkles

1 ice cream wafer

red and yellow fruit roll-ups

4 colored gum balls

sugar star decorations

NOTE

Make sure you check the package size
of the cake mix before you start and
adjust the size accordingly.

1 Preheat the oven to 350°F. Grease the cake pans and line the bases with
parchment paper. Divide the cake mix evenly between the pans and bake for
45 minutes, or until a skewer inserted into the center of the cakes comes out
clean. Let the cakes cool in the pans for 5 minutes before turning out onto a
wire rack to cool completely.

2 Leave the ring cake whole and cut a curve from one end of the loaf cake, as
shown. Arrange the cakes on the cake board in the figure nine, joining the edges
with a little buttercream. Trim to neaten the edges and the top of the cake.

3 Divide the buttercream into six even amounts. Leave one portion white, tint
one portion black, and tint the others four shades of blue, from light to dark.

4 Spread the buttercream over the cakes, starting with the lighter colors at the
bottom and moving up to the darker ones at the top. Blend each color into
the other at the edges.

5 Roll out half the ready-made frosting with a rolling pin to about ⅛ inch thick.
Cut out star shapes with a small star cutter or using a small, sharp knife. Cut
a circle for a planet.

6 To make the rocket, slice off one side of the ice cream cone so that it can sit
flat. Spread the rocket with a little white buttercream and roll it on a plate filled
with dragées and colored sprinkles. Carefully fill in any gaps—tweezers make
this job much easier. To make the wings, cut the ice cream wafer in half along
the diagonal and decorate as above. Sit the rocket's body halfway along the
straight part of the figure nine and slide a wafer wing under each side.

7 Cut the fruit roll-ups into thin strips for the flames and one thin curved strip
for the ring around the planet. Add the "flames" and the gum balls to the base
of the rocket. Sprinkle the rocket with sugar star decorations. As a final touch,
add your stars, planet, and planet's ring.

Cut a curve off the top of the loaf cake
so that it will neatly join to the ring.

Join the loaf cake to the ring cake to form
a figure nine.

Use a small knife or cutter to cut stars
out of the ready-made frosting.

Roll the cone on a plate covered with dragées and colored sprinkles.

Move one of the loaf cakes in the middle of the round cake and cut off the overhang.

Frost the palette and brush with colored buttercream.

Use tweezers to adorn the paintbrush with silver dragées.

at last! I am ten

1   Preheat the oven to 350°F. Grease the cake pans and line the bases with parchment paper. Divide the cake mix evenly among the tins and bake the loaf tins for 40 minutes and the round pan for 55 minutes, or until a skewer inserted into the center of the cakes comes out clean. Let the cakes cool in the pans for 5 minutes before turning out onto a wire rack to cool completely.

2   Level the cakes if necessary. Put the round cake on the cake board, cut it in half crosswise and move the pieces apart. Move one of the loaf cakes into the middle. Cut off the overhanging part of the loaf cake. Sit the other loaf cake to the left of the round cake and add the offcut to the bottom.

3   Join the cake pieces together with some buttercream. Put the template of the paintbrush on the loaf cake and secure with toothpicks. Mark the line between the bristles and the handle by piercing through the paper onto the cake with a skewer or toothpick. Cut to shape.

4   Put the template of the palette on the round cake and secure with toothpicks. To make the finger hole in the palette, you can either cut through the template with a sharp knife, or mark the area with a skewer and cut it out after you have removed the template.

5   Leave half the buttercream white for the palette. Put one-quarter of the remaining buttercream in a bowl and tint it caramel. Now put 1/3 cup of the buttercream in another bowl and tint it bright red. Leave the remaining buttercream white until needed. Spread the caramel buttercream over the bristles, making furrows for texture, and spread red over the handle. Spread the palette with the white buttercream.

6   Put the chocolate chips in a heatproof bowl. Bring a saucepan of water to the boil, then remove from the heat. Sit the bowl over the pan, making sure the base of the bowl does not sit in the water. Stir occasionally until the chocolate has melted. Spoon the chocolate into a piping bag. Pipe individual hairs over the brown buttercream, leaving a narrow strip at the bottom for three rows of dragées. To finish the brush, carefully put three rows of dragées between the hairs and the handle.

7   Divide the remaining buttercream into small portions and tint them different colors. Add dabs of the colors onto the palette to look like paints.

CAKE AND EQUIPMENT
8½-inch round pan
two 10 x 3 x 5 inch loaf pans
2 packages cake mix (23½ ounces)
12 x 12 inch cake board
copy of template from page 159
toothpicks or skewers

DECORATION
2 quantities buttercream from page 11
food colorings: caramel, red (we used
    powder for red), and other assorted
    colors
¼ cup chocolate chips
silver dragées

NOTE
Make sure you check the package size
of the cake mix before you start and
adjust the size accordingly.

templates

To enlarge the templates, use a photocopier to enlarge the image by the amount given. If your photocopier only enlarges to a maximum of 200%, use the measurements given in parentheses to enlarge in two steps. If you don't have access to a photocopier, draw a graph with the same size square indicated on the template, then transfer the drawing to paper.

marvin the martian

pages 18–19

100%

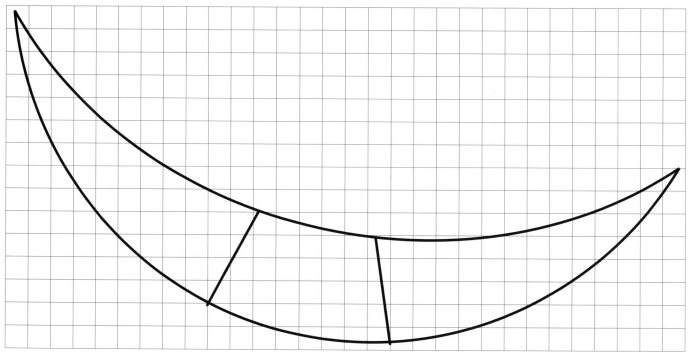

Each square = 1/4 inch

desmond the dinosaur

pages 22–23

Enlarge 260%
(200% then 130%)

Each square = ¹/₂ inch

splash! the mermaid

pages 24–25

Enlarge 300%
(200% then 150%)

Each square = ³/₄ inch

cranky witch

pages 26–27

Enlarge 166%
(150% then 111%)

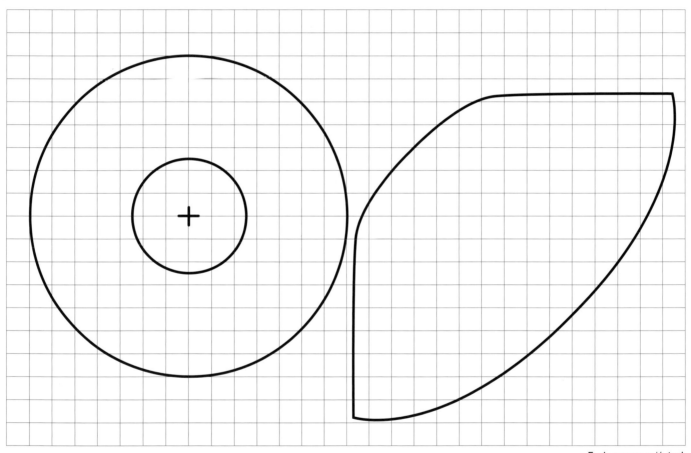

Each square = ¹/₃ inch

happy clown

pages 28–29

Enlarge 200%

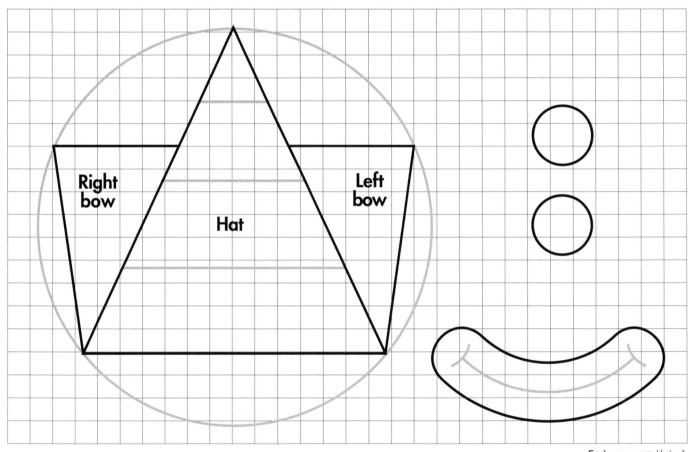

Right bow

Left bow

Hat

Each square = ¹/₂ inch

ferocious monster

pages 30–31

Enlarge 215%
(200% then 110%)

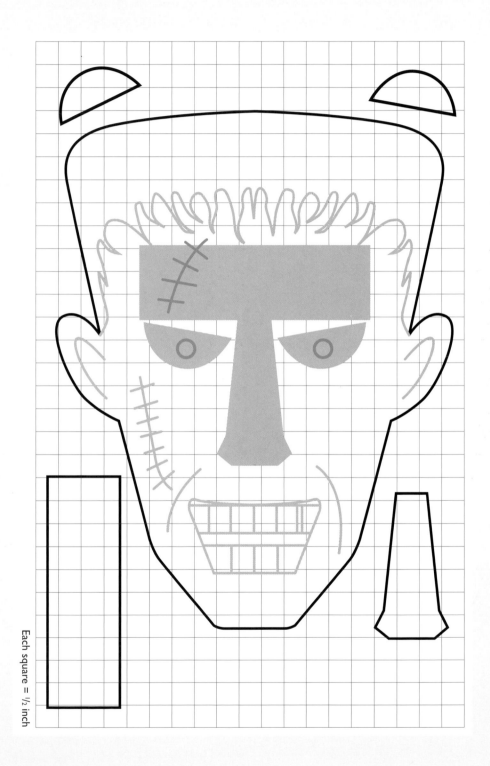

Each square = ¹/₂ inch

creepy-crawly caterpillar

pages 34–35

100%

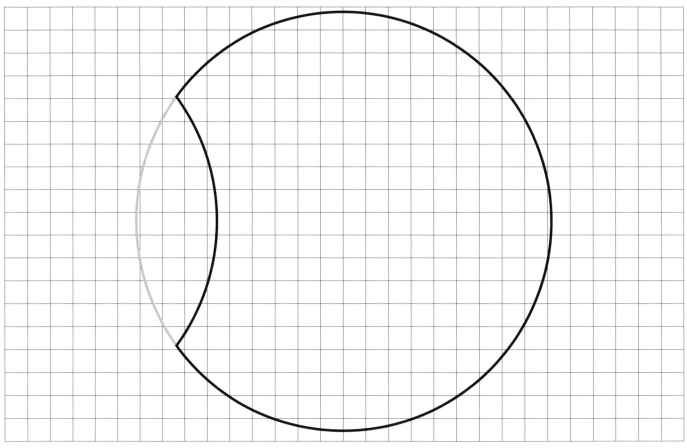

Each square = ¹/₄ inch

fresh as a daisy

pages 36–37

Enlarge 215%
(200% then 110%)

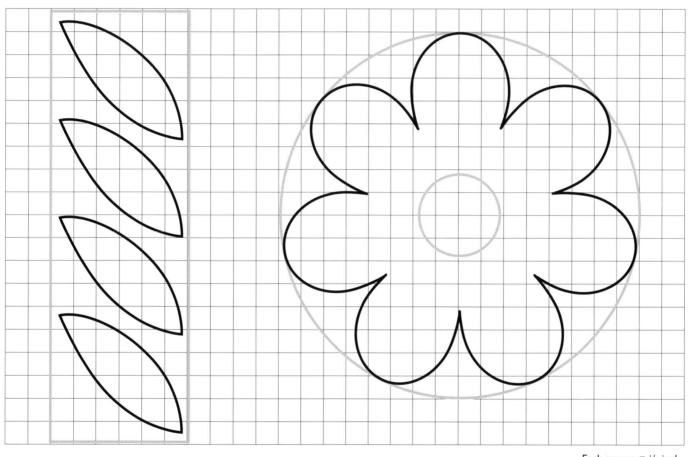

Each square = $\frac{1}{2}$ inch

hopping rabbit

pages 38–39

Enlarge 165%

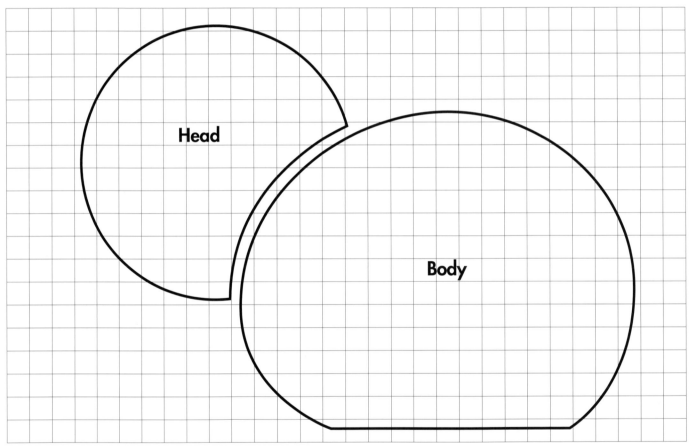

Each square = $1/3$ inch

Enlarge 165%

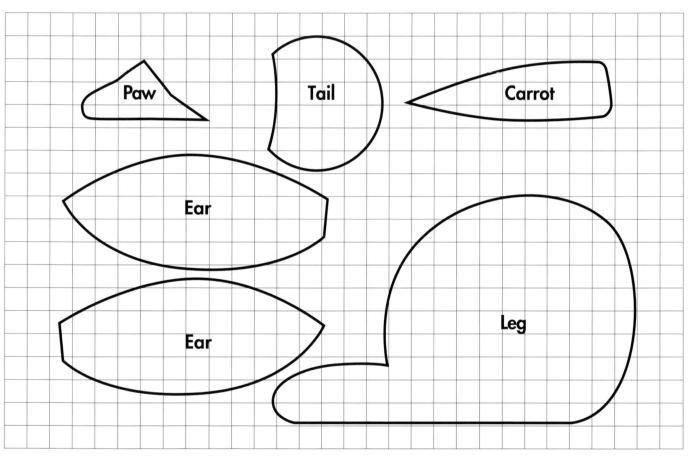

Each square = $1/3$ inch

little miss ladybird

pages 42–43

Enlarge 208%
(200% then 104%)

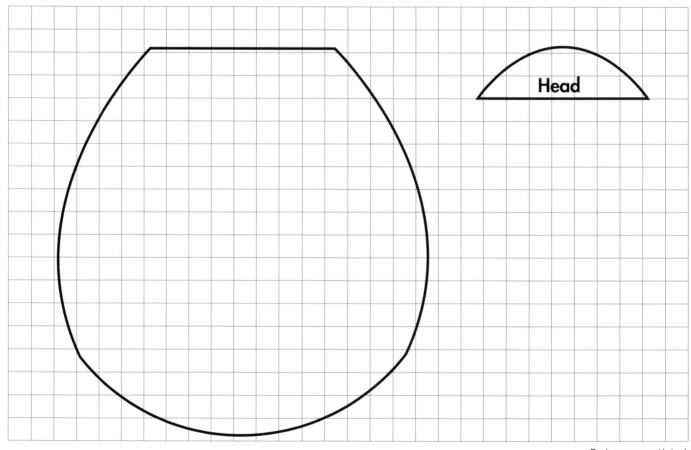

Head

Each square = ¹/₂ inch

beautiful butterfly

pages 44–45

Enlarge 165%

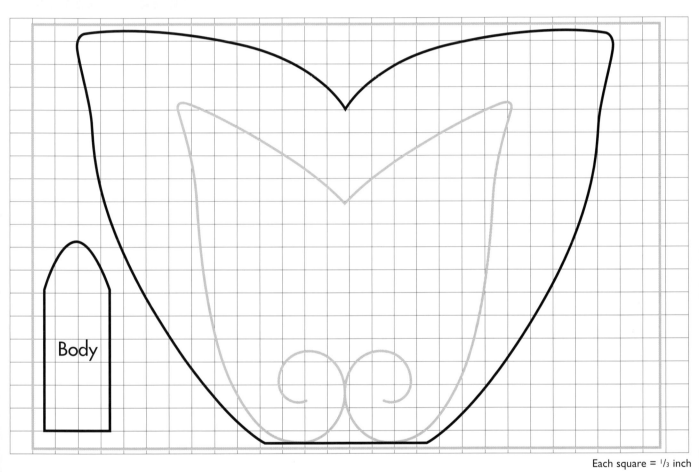

Body

Each square = $^1/_3$ inch

tropical fish

pages 46–47

Enlarge 250%
(200% then 125%)

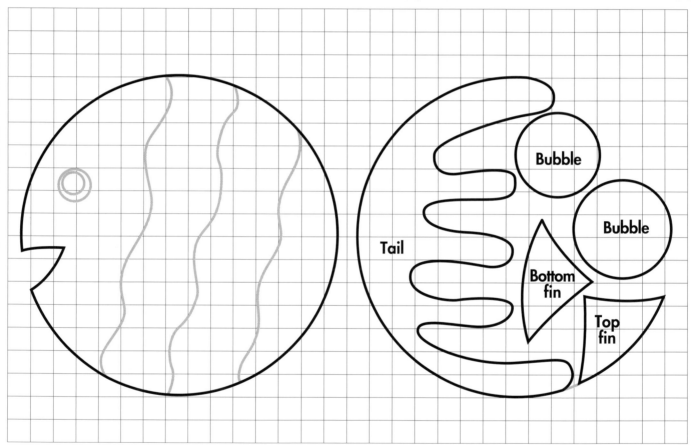

Each square = ½ inch

spotty the dog

pages 50–51

Enlarge 250%
(200% then 125%)

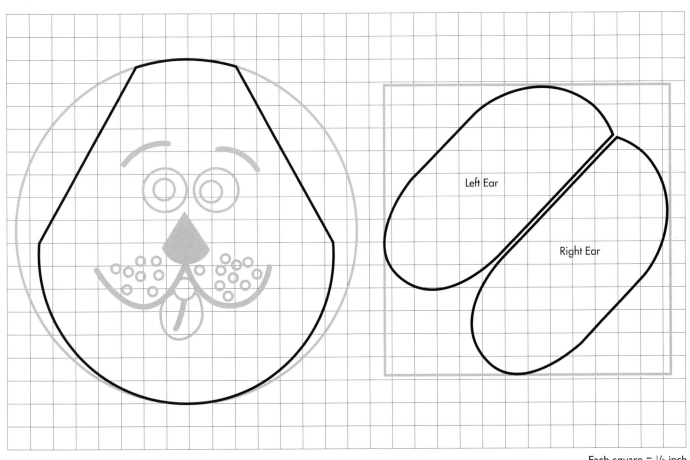

Left Ear

Right Ear

Each square = $^1/_2$ inch

cat on a mat

pages 52–53

Enlarge 215%
(200% then 110%)

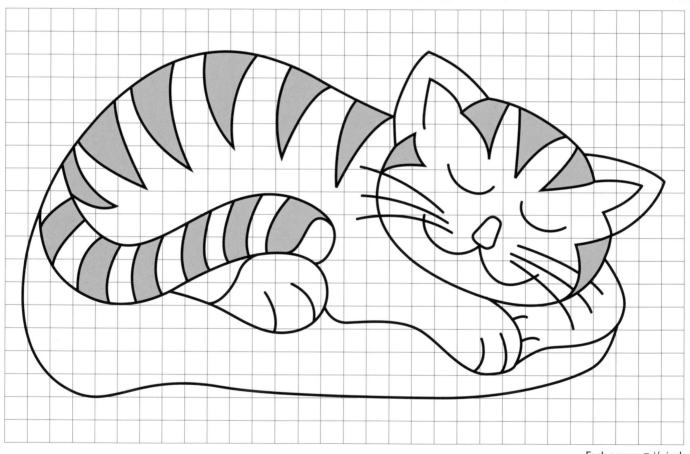

Each square = $\frac{1}{2}$ inch

fatty the whale

pages 54–55

Enlarge 266%
(200% then 133%)

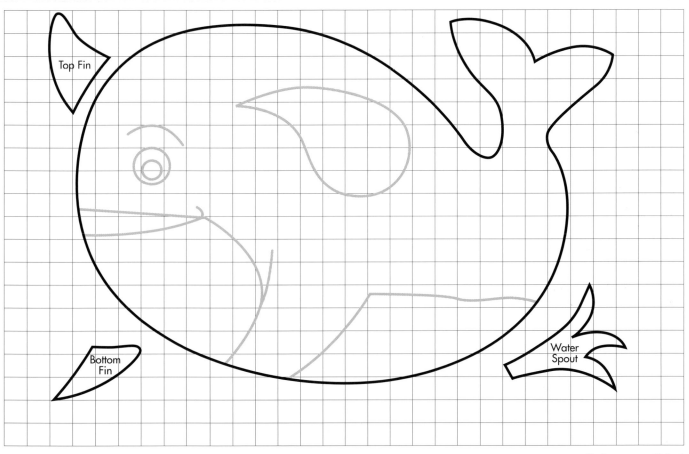

Top Fin

Bottom
Fin

Water
Spout

Each square = 1/2 inch

fighter plane

pages 62–63

Enlarge 183%

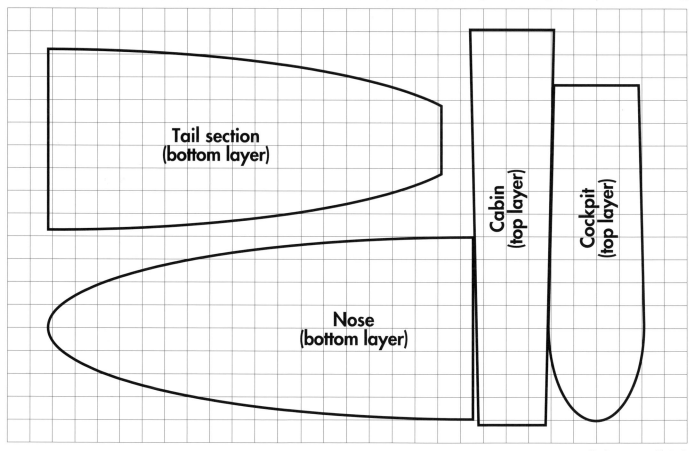

**Tail section
(bottom layer)**

**Nose
(bottom layer)**

**Cabin
(top layer)**

**Cockpit
(top layer)**

Each square = ¹/₃ inch

Enlarge 183%

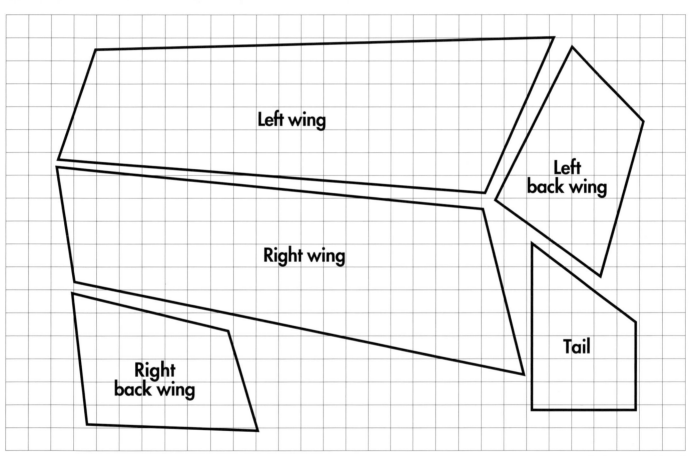

Left wing

Left
back wing

Right wing

Tail

Right
back wing

Each square = ¹/₃ inch

gnarly dude! skateboard

pages 66–67

Enlarge 165%

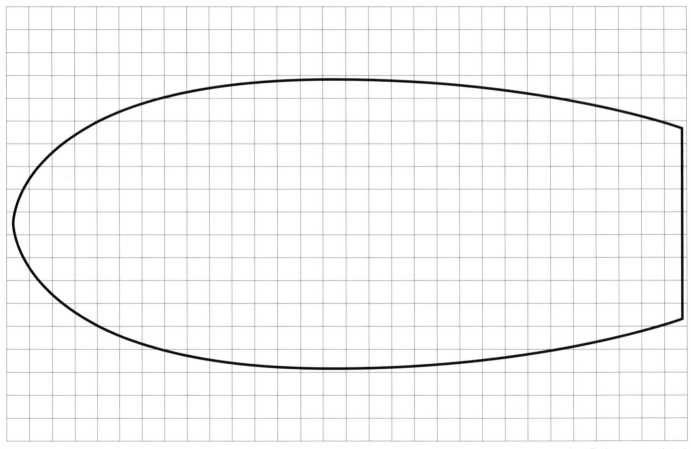

Each square = 1/3 inch

electric guitar

pages 68–69

Enlarge 215%
(200% then 110%)

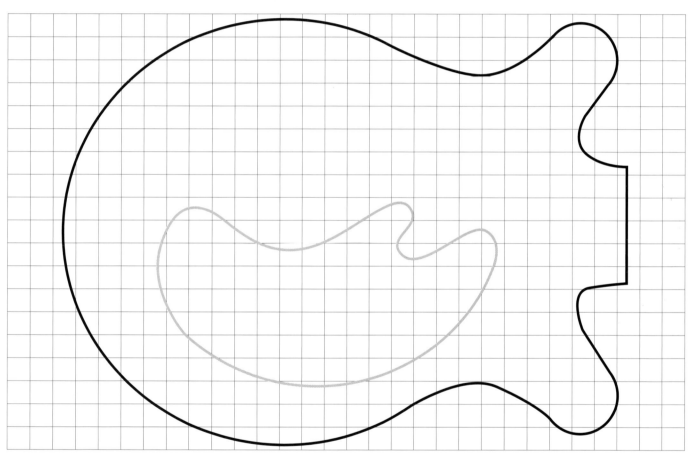

Each square = ½ inch

vroom vroom racing car

pages 70–71

Enlarge 200%

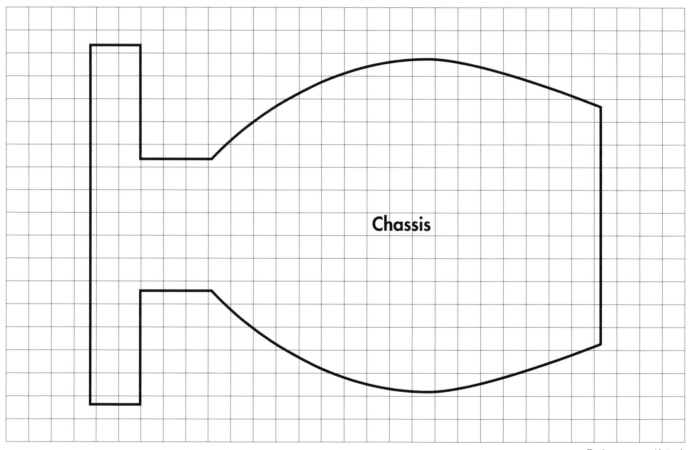

Chassis

Each square = $^1/_2$ inch

cricket bat and ball

pages 76–77

Enlarge 150%

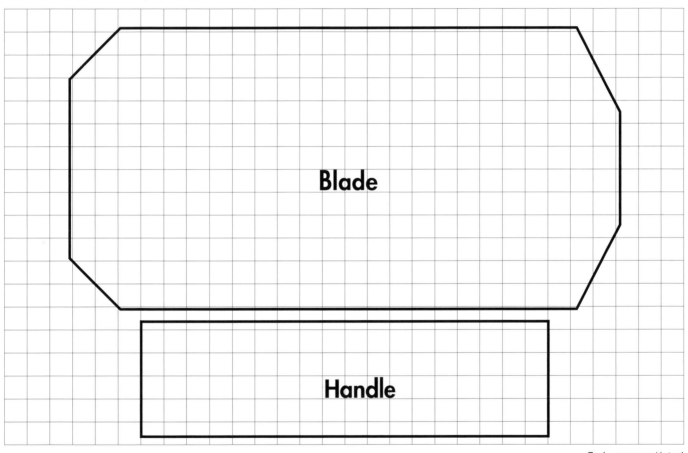

Blade

Handle

Each square = $^1/_3$ inch

bart simpson

pages 82–83

Enlarge 266%
(200% then 133%)

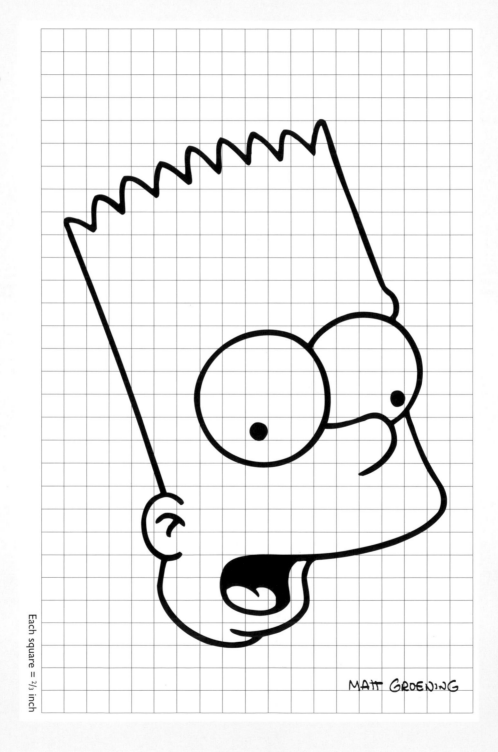

Each square = ²/₃ inch

MATT GROENING

marge simpson

pages 84–85

Enlarge 333%
(200% then 167%)

Each square = ³/₄ inch

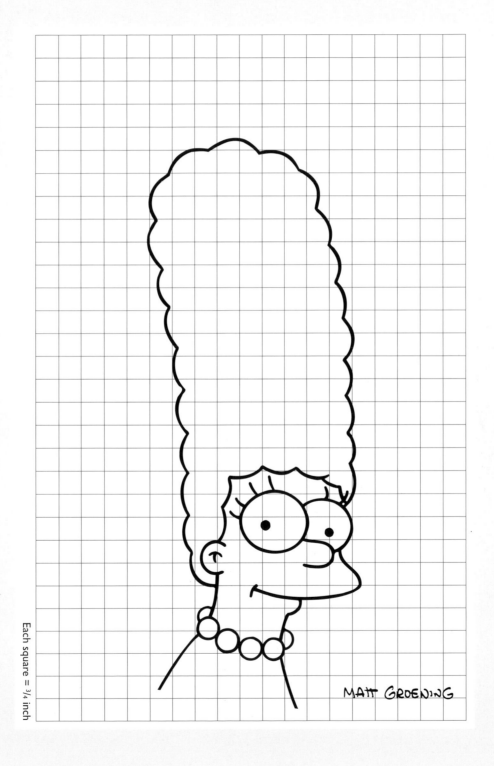

MATT GROENING

homer simpson

pages 86–87

Enlarge 283%
(200% then 142%)

Each square = 3/4 inch

MATT GROENING

lisa simpson

pages 88–89

Enlarge 283%
(200% then 142%)

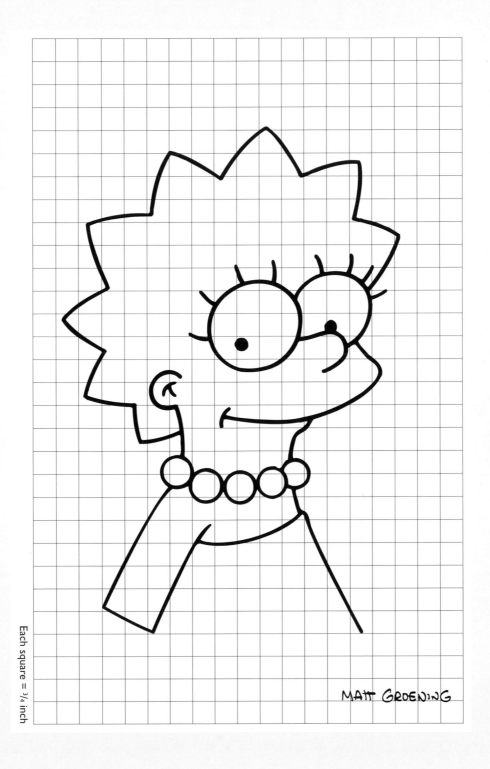

Each square = ¾ inch

maggie simpson

pages 90–91

Enlarge 283%
(200% then 142%)

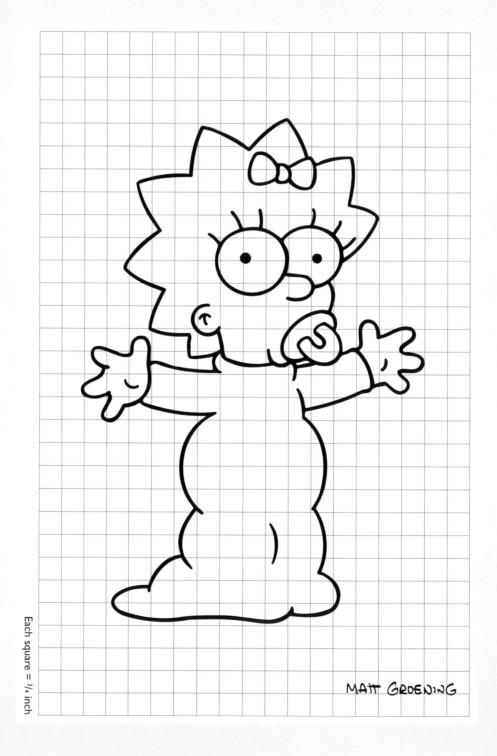

Each square = ¾ inch

MATT GROENING

santa's little helper

pages 92–93

Enlarge 283%
(200% then 142%)

Each square = ³/₄ inch

MATT GROENING

mr. montgomery burns

pages 94–95

Enlarge 266%
(200% then 133%)

Each square = ¾ inch

MATT GROENING

head to toe bart simpson

pages 96–97

Enlarge 266%
(200% then 133%)

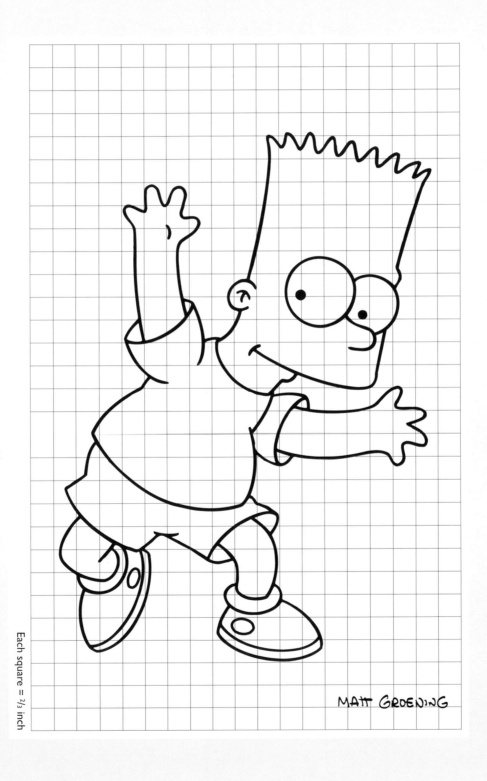

Each square = ²/₃ inch

MATT GROENING

itchy & scratchy

pages 98–99

Enlarge 300%
(200% then 150%)

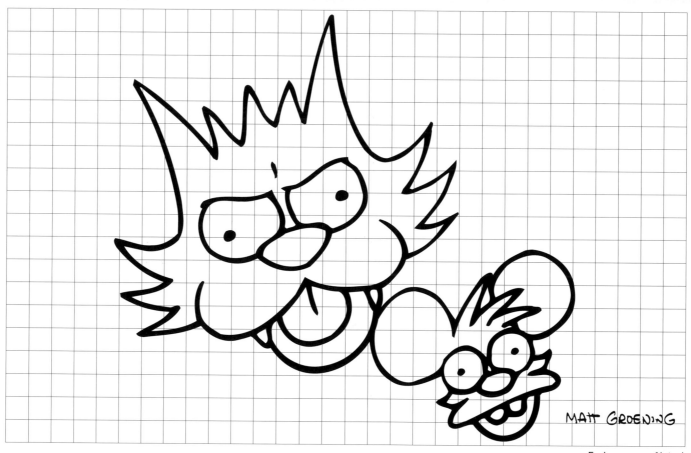

Each square = ³/₄ inch

krusty the clown

pages 100–101

Enlarge 350%
(200% then 175%)

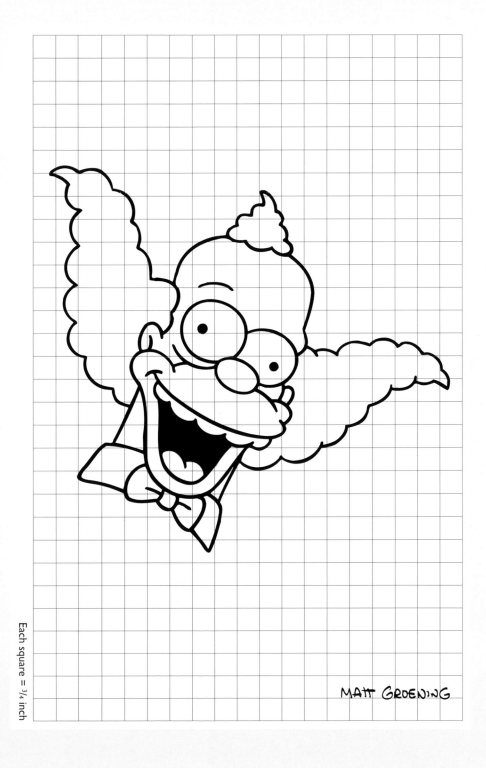

Each square = 3/4 inch

MATT GROENING

snakey number two

pages 106–107

Enlarge 215%
(200% then 110%)

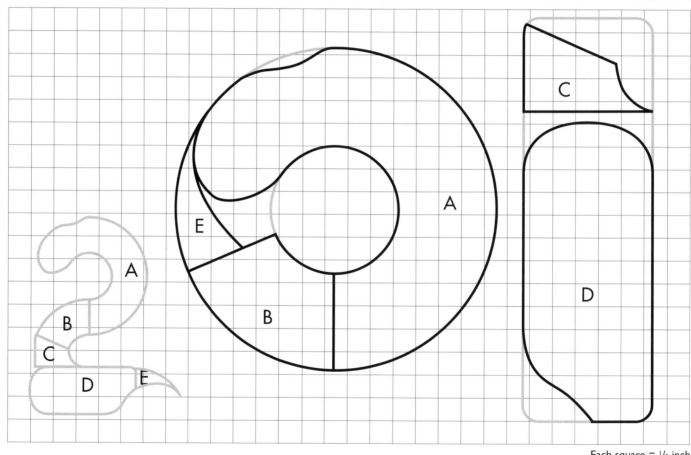

Each square = ¹/₂ inch

at last! I am ten

pages 122–123

Enlarge 266%
(200% then 133%)

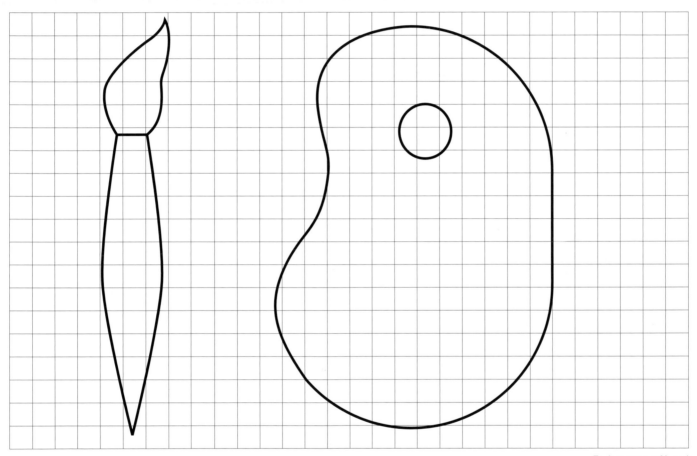

Each square = ²/₃ inch

index